STAIRWAY TO THE STARS

STAIRWAY TO THE STARS

Sufism, Gurdjieff and the Inner Tradition of Mankind

Max Gorman

AEON

First published in 2010 by
Aeon Books Ltd
118 Finchley Road
London NW3 5HT

British Library Cataloguing in Publication Data

A C.I.P. for this book is available from the British Library

ISBN-13: 978-1-90465-832-0

Typeset by Vikatan Publishing Solutions (P) Ltd., Chennai, India

www.aeonbooks.co.uk

O silver trumpets, be you lifted up
And cry to the great race that is to come.
Long-throated swans among the waves of time
Sing loudly, for beyond the wall of the world
It waits, and it may hear, and come to us.

W.B. Yeats

ACKNOWLEDGEMENTS

I am grateful to Aubrey Wolton who suggested, and encouraged me to write this book.

I also wish to thank Cathy Shepherd for her patient and excellent typing of the manuscript.

CONTENTS

CHAPTER ONE

Prelude

We are born, we live, we die. Not really understanding what these experiences really mean. We come—we know not whence? We stay—we know not why? And we go—we know not whither?

But while we are here, whatever and wherever 'here' really is, we live, or believe we live—whatever we mean by that. For indeed it may be, as the Sufi mystics claim, that 'It is a fundamental mistake of man's to think that he is alive—when he has merely fallen asleep in Life's waiting room.'

Nevertheless, we do experience something, the state and experiences we call 'life', with all its joys and sorrows, sunsets and sunrises, storms and calms, delights and disturbances, dreams, and its *sleeps*. For are there not times when each of us feels that sense of being asleep—which the mystics might be referring to—when we have more than a suspicion that we are not really awake, that life is tinged with unreality, that we live as but a shadow of our self, and see only 'Through a glass, darkly, but never face to face'?

> O what can ail thee, Knight-at-arms,
> Alone and palely loitering?

> The sedge has wither'd from the lake,
> And no birds sing.

Do we not all recognise that grey and songless twilight of the soul? Have we not all loitered by that lake? And known that the Knight's question is *our* question? What aileth *us*?

And are we not more like Tennyson's Lotus Eaters than we would care to admit, drowsily drifting through large parts of our life in a somnolent trance, a meaningless miasma? And, like the Lady of Shalott, do we not also cry in our hearts when we are alone, 'I am half-sick of shadows!'

For some of us yearn, consciously or unconsciously, for some other kind of life, qualitatively superior, more real, richer, more intense, than the one we are presented with. This thing so dramatically called 'life' contents us not. We are restless. There is a profound discontent, a deep disquiet in our souls. We do not know why. As Tennyson expresses it:

> Tears, idle tears, I know not what they mean
> Tears from the depth of some divine despair …

We sometimes suspect that the life we normally encounter might be as shadow to substance, trance to truth. There is something deep within us that refuses to die, that dreams of something beyond the confines of ordinary life—a strange unfading faith in a higher existence, a richer reality. We feel an unfulfilment, a yearning in the heart's heart, a sense of loss for something, somewhere, sometime … we know not what?

Perhaps a piece of music, a haunting melody, a painting, a poem, or an experience of nature, may evoke, may remind us, may communicate something special to us. But the music over, we return to our slumber. Yet, as Walter De La Mare tells us:

> Very old are we men;
> Our dreams are tales
> Told in dim Eden
> By Eve's nightingales.

For some dreams we dream are the dreams of awakening. They are the Call from the World of the Awake. In the words of a Gnostic text:

I am the Voice of Awakening from Sleep
In the Aeon of the Night.

Or, in early Christian words, 'Awake, thou that *sleepest*, and arise from the dead, and Christ shall give thee light.'

And what can this 'light' be but the richer, fuller life, our very Birthright—which the Nazarene master must be referring to when he says, (John 10:10) 'I am come that they might have life, and that they might have it more abundantly.'

And when the playwright, Ibsen, entitled one of his works 'When We Dead Awaken'—was this not also a dim adumbrance of the same thing, a hint of our higher possibilities, a dream of our inner destiny—which makes us forever restless?

Some of us indeed are graced with mystical experiences, and enter states of consciousness of a higher, fuller kind, in which for a time, or an eternity—for those who have experienced such states say they leave time behind—the world appears different, more beautiful, radiant, mysteriously interwoven with another finer, higher world or worlds, where Earth is seen to be somehow encompassed by Heaven, with which it is seen to be connected, and by which it is sustained and upheld. The Universe is, after all, despite appearances, One—yet vividly various, and iridescent with individuality! The ancient Sumerians were, it seems, right. The Universe is indeed 'an-ki', as they called it, meaning 'heaven-earth'. And so too was John Eringena, the ninth century philosopher, when he said, 'Visibilia ex Invisibiliis'—the visible comes from the invisible. Which relationship the poet John Masefield must have once vividly perceived to have written:

> The station brook to my new eyes
> Was babbling out of Paradise.
> The waters rushing from the rain
> Were singing Christ is risen again.
> I thought all earthly creatures knelt
> For rapture of the joy I felt.
> The narrow station wall's brick ledge
> The wild hop withering in the hedge.
> The lights in huntsman's upper storey
> Were parts of an eternal glory.

While Thomas Traherne, the seventeenth century mystic, describes a similar experience in these words:

> All things abided eternally, as they were in their proper place. Eternity was manifest in the light of day, and something infinite behind everything appeared.

'Man can perceive more than sense can discover.' said Blake, who believed that man is 'encaverned' here on earth when he is born, by the five senses; and so, in one of his poems, the soul descending into the body cries, 'They told me I had five senses to enclose me up.'

Here Blake concurs with the mystics, who claim that our five ordinary senses can act as a barrier to the inner senses we also possess, with their own inner vision. This indeed is to him and certain other mystics the real meaning of 'the Fall'. It is the fall *outwards* from within. There are, he says, two worlds; the external world we normally encounter and identify ourselves with; and the world within, which he refers to as 'The Kingdom not of this world', using, significantly, the same term as Jesus. This inner world is accessible only to an inner perception. Hence Blake's words under his engraving, 'What is Man?'

> The Sun's Light when he unfolds it
> Depends on the organ that beholds it.

'As a man is, so he sees,' he says. For Blake understood what Gurdjieff more recently tried to communicate, that perception depends on being. They are both organically related. 'I have more to tell you but ye cannot contain it now.' (John 16:12) said the Nazarene master on the same subject. Consciousness must be 'carried' by being. And it is the deliberate cultivation of being and consciousness that is the aim of the mystic.

I repeat, *deliberate*. For however wonderful are the experiences some people have on rare and special occasions received, and others more frequently due to particular gifts and qualities they possess 'by nature', I am here primarily concerned with the possibility of the conscious and deliberate development of perception, of the acquisition of higher consciousness as a permanent state in man, accompanied, as it must be, by the development and transformation of his very being. This, therefore, goes beyond mysticism as usually understood, for the accent is not on special experience or revelation, but rather on the attainment, through effort and education, of a different and higher kind of *life*.

This, indeed, is, and always has been, the education given to those who sincerely seek it, by the true mystical schools, and it is to them that we shall particularly turn in our search. The whole concept of such a school may be strange to many of us. Yet it will be more than submitted that the role of such entities has been, and continues to be, of central significance to the survival and evolution of the human race.

CHAPTER TWO

The message of the mystic

From time immemorial, certain men and women appear to have developed their consciousness far beyond the 'normal' level or state which the rest of humanity has taken for granted as 'life'. These are the mystics. They are of all times and places, of the East as well as the West. They emerge from every religion or none. For theirs is a spiritual rather than a religious quest. Religion, derived from the Latin 'religio'—to bind—does just that, confusing morality with spirituality, doctrine with development. It is not belief that matters to the mystic, but experience—personal, inner experience. Then belief is replaced by knowledge—direct spiritual knowledge.

The true mystics are not culture-bound. They have gone 'beyond'. They may well have to take into consideration the prevailing culture for purposes of communication. But their message is for mankind. Or more accurately, for those human beings who are seeking, those who will listen. In the words of one mystical master, 'those who have ears to hear'. It is the ultimate human message, from ultimate human beings. It is the deep calling to the deep in us. If our hearts can but hear!

The mystic originates from all places, yet he becomes placeless. In the words of the great Sufi adept, Jalaluddin Rumi:

> I am not of the East, nor of the West;
> Not of the land, not of the sea;
> Neither of this world, nor of the next;
> My place is placeless, my trace traceless.

Rumi is saying his only abode is Reality. And when Jesus of Nazareth informs us, 'The foxes have their holes and the birds have nests, but the son of man has nowhere to rest his head.' (Matthew 8:20) he is surely communicating the same thing.

Again, though the mystic is from all times, he is timeless. His state is timeless, his experience is timeless, he has moved beyond time. 'Be above time.' Says Jesus in the little known Gospel of Mary discovered in Akmim, Upper Egypt in 1895, indicating, like other mystical masters, the supratemporal nature of the state of being he called the 'Kingdom of Heaven', the attainment of which was the central purpose of his teaching.

We are referring, therefore, to the possible availability of a special kind of teaching offered by certain mystics, who are also *teachers* (a rare breed), to enable other human beings to climb the stairway which they have already ascended, to a higher level of existence. Such teaching must necessarily be of a subtle and sophisticated nature, requiring effort and receptivity on the part of the student. It is as much a *learning* as it is a teaching.

This then is 'the Way', which means both a path, and the way of following it. And if it is to lead us to a higher level of being and intelligence than we ordinarily possess, then it is clear that it must be designed and directed by one who is already that higher kind of being. Only a man or woman who has already travelled the Path, who has been that way before, can help him or her who seeks to follow after. Only such a person can provide the constant conscious surveillance necessary. Otherwise at best the journey will not begin—however much it might appear to; or at worst, end in a crevasse a foot or so away—however much it might not appear to!

But the Message of the Mystic is an optimistic one. Man has potential beyond his dreams. So much so that his dreams may even inhibit this potential. If he learns to develop himself, 'he will be able to increase his existence infinitely. If he does not, he may dwindle to vanishing point.' Such is the importance of this kind of education according to Ustad Hilmi, an adept of Central Asia. He is a Sufi mystic and this statement by him entitled 'The Sufi Quest' is recorded by Idries Shah in his book *'Thinkers of the East'*:

> Man originates from far away; so far indeed that in speaking of his origin such phrases as 'beyond the stars' are frequently employed. Man is estranged from his origins. Some of his feelings are indicators of this. Dimly he senses this separation, this exile.
>
> Man, in fact, has the opportunity of returning to his origin. He has forgotten this. He is thus 'asleep' to the reality.
>
> Sufism is designed as the means to help awaken man to the realisation, not just the opinion, of the above statements. Those who awaken are able to return, to start the journey, while also living this present life in all its fullness.
>
> People have been sent, from time to time, to try to serve man and save him form his 'blindness' and 'sleep' (which today would be better described as 'amnesia'). These people have always been in touch with the Origin, whose agents they are. They have been of all races, and of all faiths.
>
> They have always had two main objectives: to show the man himself as he really is; and to help him develop his real, inner self, his permanent part.
>
> Thus though man originates from far away, and is asleep, he can return if he attains the means to do so.

I often quote the Sufi mystics because it seems to me that they are able to provide us with extremely clear statements upon this subject—which can be considered to be no less than the very purpose of life itself. Another Sufi says:

> Humanity was created for a purpose, knew what this purpose was before assuming the human form, forgot what this was at the point of birth, can start to remember it given appropriate 'reminders', and continues to exists after physical death in a state which has been modified by the terrestrial phase.

Wordsworth indeed expresses insight into this situation when he says:

> Our birth is but a sleep and a forgetting:
> The soul that rises from within us, our life's star,
> Hath had elsewhere its setting,
> And cometh from afar.

The Sufi and other mystics would agree with the poet. But the Sufi insists that unless this 'sleep' and this 'forgetting' is overcome *here* and *now* during our planetary existence, the 'immortality' of which Wordsworth here speaks in this his '*Ode on Intimations of Immortality from Recollections of Early Childhood*' will be of a lesser kind, will lack the quality of being that can only be acquired by the developmental work, the deliberate and conscious spiritual evolution, for which this terrestrial phase is both the opportunity and the medium. If this is not done, life after death will be little better than life before death. For 'Where your heart is, there will your heaven be.'

CHAPTER THREE

Towards the recognition of sleep

Mystics might say we are asleep—but why should we believe them? After all, we all know what sleep is—it is what we do at night when we lie in bed. And in the morning we wake, get up, dress, and then proceed to do all the many, varied and often complicated things that occupy our 'waking hours'. How can we possibly be asleep if we can constantly and successfully perform such activities as hold conversations, cross roads, read books, bring up children, and keep our jobs?

This is a perfectly fair question, based as it is on a fair assumption. It does indeed *seem* that we are awake on the criterion of what we do and achieve in our daily life. Everything appears to support that belief, or rather, as the mystic would say, conspires to maintain that notion. Yet it is surprising what 'real' sleepwalkers can in fact do in their sleep (apart from going up and down stairs safely). Some have held intelligent conversations—which they have entirely forgotten later. There is even a report of someone coming down from his bedroom to play a fairly difficult piece on the piano before an audience of his friends, who had been talking late. He remembered nothing of his performance in the morning.

11

It is, of course, accepted that there is a difference between sleep at night, and our state during the day, when we do all the things we have to do in order to survive, and more. But the question has nevertheless to be asked, how awake do we really have to be to adequately perform so much of what we habitually perform every day, and which we take for granted we are performing consciously?

Admittedly, we are all aware from time to time, though perhaps not as often as we should be, of doing things and saying things 'automatically'. This is an important observation, when indeed we have it, with considerable implication if we but allowed ourselves to fully register and ponder it. But connected with this is an extremely significant feature of our ordinary consciousness of which most of us are entirely *unaware*, and which indeed indicates that we are very much more asleep than we imagine ourselves to be. Though referred to by the Sufis both directly and indirectly, it was the mystical teacher George Ivanovitch Gurdjieff who most clearly and insistently pointed out this curious and considerable defect in ordinary human consciousness, to remedy which was a central part of his work with his pupils.

I say 'curious' because it is indeed odd that so major and fundamental a feature of human consciousness, or more accurately *lack* of it, and because of which so many of our defects can be derived, has totally escaped our observation, and continues to do so. I refer to our almost permanent lack of *self*-consciousness. Now in order to understand what this means, let us look closely at the situation with Gurdjieff and his pupils at St. Petersburg in 1915, when he first attempts to communicate this concept to them. I quote from Ouspensky's account of the occasion as recorded in his book '*In Search of the Miraculous*':

> On one occasion, at the beginning of a meeting, G put a question to which all of us present had to answer in turn. The question was: 'What is the most important thing that we notice during self-observation?'
>
> Some of those present said that during attempts at self-observation what they had felt particularly strongly was an incessant flow of thoughts, which they had found impossible to stop. Others spoke of the difficulty of distinguishing the work of one centre from the work of another. (Gurdjieff taught that the

human being had three 'centres': the emotional, the thinking, and the moving centre.)

G was obviously dissatisfied with our replies. I had already begun to understand him in such circumstances and I saw that he expected from us indications of something that we had either missed or failed to understand.

'Not one of you has noticed the most important thing that I have pointed out to you,' he said. 'That is to say not one of you has noticed that *you do not remember yourselves.*' (He gave particular emphasis to these words.) 'You do not feel *yourselves,* you are not *conscious* of *yourselves.* You do not feel: *I* observe, I speak, I see. With you, everything 'is observed', 'is spoken', 'is seen'. In order really to observe oneself, one must first all *remember oneself.*' (He again emphasised these words.) 'Try to *remember yourselves* when you observe yourselves and later on tell me the results. Only those results will have any value that are accompanied by self-remembering. Otherwise you yourselves do not exist in your observations. In which case, what are all your observations worth?'

These words of G's made me think a great deal. It seemed to me at once that they were the key to what he had said before about consciousness. But I decided to draw no conclusions whatsoever, but to try to *remember myself* while observing myself.

The very first attempts showed me how difficult it was. Attempts at self-remembering failed to give any results except to show me that in actual fact we *never* remember ourselves.

'What else do you want?' said G. 'this is a very important realisation. People who *know this*' (he emphasised these words) 'already know a great deal. The whole trouble is that nobody knows it. If you ask a man whether he can remember himself he will of course answer that he can. If you tell him that he cannot remember himself, he will either be angry with you, or he will think you an utter fool. The whole of human life is based on this, the whole of human existence, the whole of human blindness. If a man really knows that he cannot remember himself, he is already near to the understanding of his being.

I have quoted this passage at length because I believe it to be of the very greatest importance. The fact that we do not in the normal course of events remember ourselves, are not properly conscious of ourselves in these events, are thus not really *present* in them, is a clear indication that we are asleep—as the mystics claim. If this disturbs, then that is a very good thing. For it is disturbing us from our sleep.

Ouspensky then also makes the following interesting observation:

> I realised that moments of self-remembering do occur in life, although rarely. Actually, I had been familiar with them from early childhood. They came either in new and unexpected surroundings, in a new place, among new people while travelling, for instance, when one suddenly looks about one and says, 'How strange I, and in this place'; or in very emotional moments, in moments of danger, in moments when it is necessary to keep one's head, when one hears one's own voice, and sees and observes oneself from the outside.

Nevertheless, these are exceptional moments. Ouspensky concludes:

> European and Western psychology have overlooked a fact of tremendous importance, namely that we do not remember ourselves; that we live and act in deep sleep, not metaphorically but in absolute reality. And also that, at the same time, we *can* remember ourselves if we make sufficient efforts, that we can awaken.

The state of consciousness which Gurdjieff calls 'self-remembering', and which we do not realise we generally lack, but which we wrongly assume we have, is not easy to describe. Communication on this subject is, for some reason, and from my personal experience, peculiarly difficult. Few people appear to be able to accept that they are not conscious of themselves in this way; that they go about doing things, saying things, seeing things and hearing things without being present in, without being aware of themselves in, these activities. That it is, not *I* do this, *I* see this, *I* hear this, even *I* think this; but rather a case of do this, see this, hear this, and think this, without the consciousness of *I* as present in the act. Most of the time and in most of our actions we are not present unto ourselves. We are absent. Or 'asleep'. It is the master's voice without the master. The master is not at home.

'Is anyone there?' said the Traveller
As he knocked at the old oak door.

The reply for most of us most of the time to that question in De La Mare's poem must be 'No'. While we have in our culture the term 'presence of mind', significantly we do not have the term 'presence of *self*'. For such absence, absence of self, is never suspected. But if it is true—surely this is a very serious matter? And could of itself account for a great many of our faults, failings and mistakes. For lack of self-presence means lack of control, lack of direction. As one Sufi advises, 'Next time you go out take your face with you. Or somebody might steal it!'

I have said that, I, like Ouspensky, have usually found it difficult to communicate to people, even those interested in mystical development, the fact that they do not remember themselves, are not aware of themselves, are not self-aware in this sense through most of their experience, through most of their existence. Many are quite unable to grasp what is meant at all. Others are confident that they are already fully in possession of this state—exactly as Gurdjieff predicted. They are insulted that you should even query or doubt it. Are you daring to suggest that they are sleepwalking? Indeed I am. It has also become clear to me that the people who regard self-consciousness as their normal possession have not only, like the former group, failed to understand what is meant by this state, but are, in fact, even further precluded from such understanding by this belief.

Ouspensky, after trying in vain to communicate this concept to certain of his friends and others who he had fully expected would be able to perceive it, says, 'I subsequently became convinced that this idea was hidden by an impenetrable veil from many otherwise intelligent people.' My own experience in this area compels me to concur.

Here is an exercise, which I hope will communicate to the reader what 'self-remembering' means:

While looking at any object in front of you, a book, a pencil, watch or window-sill—it doesn't really matter what—gradually and *simultaneously* become conscious, become aware of your *self*, your 'I' looking at *it*. In other words, you are going inwards, entering in, to feel 'I' looking out at, seeing *it*. You must never lose, you must fully and constantly sustain this sense of *you* looking at *it*. Thus *you* are fully *present* in looking. The perceiver is present *in* the perceiving of the thing perceived. The perceiver perceives himself perceiving the thing perceived.

You will find it difficult to do this at all at first. And once you have achieved it, difficult to continue for more than a minute or so. You will tend to repeatedly forget yourself and simply become immersed in seeing, without the requisite simultaneous awareness of yourself as the seer. But encountering this very difficulty is in itself a significant step. For it indicates that self-remembering is not something you normally do. It is a new and different experience. And requires a particular effort of consciousness on your part to achieve. This is valuable knowledge. For you have now recognised a major aspect of your sleep.

While lack of self-consciousness is an element in our sleep, the *possession* of it represents in fact a higher state of consciousness than the 'normal'. Gurdjieff described it as 'the *third* state of consciousness'. The first being asleep in bed; the second being our ordinary state of consciousness. He stressed that without the acquisition of this third state of consciousness, self-remembering, it was not possible to ascend to the highest state of consciousness, the ultimate aim of the mystical quest, which he called 'the fourth state of consciousness'. To quote Gurdjieff's words:

> Man, by which I mean fully developed man, should and does possess four states of consciousness. But ordinary man lives in two states of consciousness only. He knows, or at least he can know of the fourth state of consciousness, which is referred to by various names in various teachings. But man does not know of the third state of consciousness or even suspect it. Nor can he suspect it because if you were to explain to him what the third state of consciousness is, that is to say, in what it consists, he would say that is was his usual state. By considering that he possesses self-consciousness, as it were by nature, a man will not, of course, try to approach or obtain it. And yet without self-consciousness, or the third state, the fourth, except in rare flashes, is impossible.

That last statement seems to me to be of very considerable importance, and tells us of something which has never before been expressed in mystical literature. That there is a third state of consciousness which is an essential prerequisite of, and an indispensable stage towards, the attainment of the highest level. So apart from its great value in itself, the third state is thus a necessary link between ordinary consciousness and the highest consciousness.

This is significant knowledge, and has doubtless always been possessed by genuine mystical schools, but for some reason has only been clearly communicated by G.I. Gurdjieff.

'What I say unto you I say unto all: *Watch.'* This instruction by Jesus reported by Mark at Chapter Thirteen, verse 37, of his Gospel, may well be relevant. The Greek work here translated as 'watch', 'gregoreite', has the fuller meaning 'be watchfully awake'. But we lack the necessary information on how to properly understand and how to fulfil this instruction that the master must have also supplied to his pupils. Which, of course, must be the case with many other of his exhortations and statements, recorded as they are in the Gospels—devoid of their full teaching context. There is a strong possibility, however, that he is talking about 'self-remembering'.

I have concentrated for so long on the subject of self-consciousness because firstly by realising its absence and our lack of it in our lives we can clearly ascertain for ourselves and identify a significant aspect of our sleep; and secondly that this realisation should begin to *disturb* this sleep, and provoke us to make efforts towards the attainment of this state of being aware of oneself in all we do, which is indeed the beginning of awakening.

Nevertheless, as has been already indicated, the sleep which the mystics say we are in is greater and more complex than only the self-forgetfulness just described, however serious a deficiency of our consciousness it undoubtedly is. For even if we possessed the third state of consciousness, as we should do fully and permanently, we would still be, according to them, only partially awake. We would still be asleep to our true potentiality, asleep in that we would not yet be in possession of that higher realm of consciousness possible to us, which the ancients called 'Wisdom', which the Mystery Schools called 'Vision', which Jesus called 'The Kingdom of Heaven', which the Gnostics called 'Gnosis', which the Illuminati called 'Illumination', termed 'The Fourth State' by Gurdjieff, and 'Perception of Knowledge' by the Sufis.

Without this state of consciousness, of being, of very life, we cannot be said to be, cannot rightly regard ourselves to be, truly conscious beings, fully responsible and responsive to our real role in this Universe. We might exist in it; but have not yet become *members* of it. And as much as such inwardly involved and fully conscious participation is a desirable state of living, so much is the mystical quest both necessary endeavour, and High Adventure.

CHAPTER FOUR

The meaning of esotericism

A proper understanding of 'esotericism' is essential in the discussion of higher human development. Because of the confusion and misunderstanding that surrounds this concept, it is necessary to clarify its meaning.

'Esoteric' means 'inner'. It comes from the Greek word 'esoteros', 'inner', and 'esos', 'in'. From the developmental point of view, 'inner' means guidance, work, and growth related to inner perception. Inner also means hidden, not necessarily deliberately, but because of its very *nature*—being accessible only to the inner faculties, and, by virtue of such nature, out of sight of and thus inaccessible to, outer or exoteric perception. 'Exoteric' is derived from the Greek 'exoteros' meaning 'outer' and 'exos', 'out'. Something esoteric is thus beyond the perception of the outer, veiled to its view, and in this sense, 'secret'.

The concept of secret in this sense is expressed by Louis Palmer in his unusual book 'Adventures in Afghanistan', when with regard to his encounter in that country with the Dervish or Sufi teaching he says:

> There is said to be a secret contained in the Dervish teaching, which is probably why these people have attracted so much

attention and interest. The Master explained to me, however, that 'secret' means something which is hidden within the real self of man, and it can only be developed, and is not the sort of secret that can be imparted to those who are not ready for it.

This explains the Sufi aphorism given to us by the contemporary Western master, Idries Shah: 'The Secret protects itself.'

Esoteric knowledge can be regard as of two kinds. Firstly, there is the higher or inner cosmic knowledge possessed by those beings who have reached the deepest levels of consciousness possible to mankind. These people are the inner or esoteric Circle of Humanity. They will obviously possess knowledge of the inner nature and destiny of the Universe related to, and necessary for, their special role in it, and which is an attribute of their level of being. It will be knowledge of the Design and the Direction of the Universe, its Purpose, and the path to that Purpose. It will connect glow-worm and galaxy, man and angel. For, as Francis Thompson wonderfully expressed it:

> All things, by immortal power
> Near or far
> Hiddenly
> To each other linked are,
> That thou can'st not stir a flower
> Without troubling of a star.

Such must be the subtle quality of knowledge possessed by beings of this order. They will be aware of the invisible Web, and in touch with its essential texture.

Secondly, there is the esoteric knowledge pertaining to the ways and schools deliberately created by this Conscious Circle, to enable those ordinary human beings who truly seek it to have access to the superior levels of being and consciousness. This is the knowledge of the manner of human development, the art of transformation itself.

In other words teaching—knowledge, or esoteric education. Clearly knowledge of such a kind, of the means of raising man's very being beyond its normal level, can only itself originate from a higher level, from which it is sent down like a ladder for ordinary humanity to recognise, grasp and mount. It should be obvious that such help, from a higher level of intelligence and surveillance is essential to the inner evolution of mankind. It is expressed in the creation, maintenance and direction of esoteric or evolutionary schools. And this kind of direction can only be given by those who are conscious of the wide and deep cosmic context of the activity. There must be an organic connection and continuum between inner cosmic knowledge and the work of schools. For the Universe is One.

This connection is, I suggest, indicated by Gurdjieff in describing a characteristic of the particular activity upon which he and his pupils were engaged, which he called 'The Fourth Way'.

> The fourth way is never without some work of a definite significance, is never without some *undertaking* around which and in connection with which it can alone exist. When this work is finished, that is to say, when the aim set before it has been accomplished, the fourth way disappears, that is, disappears from a given place, disappears in its given form, continuing perhaps in another place in another form. Schools of the fourth way exist for the needs of the work which is being carried out in connection with the proposed undertaking.

Though it is true that esoteric means secret in the sense described, it is nevertheless also true that esoteric schools have, on the whole, through the course of human history and depending on the nature of their cultural contexts, been secret in the usual sense. The main reason for this secrecy is protection. There are two salient aspects to this question.

Firstly, it may be necessary to keep secret the nature or very existence of such a school in order to protect it from a surrounding culture which would normally be hostile to it through fear, ignorance, and suspicion; in particular when a society contained a hierarchy or hierarchies which would regard the esoteric organisation as a threat to their power, image and identity. Catholic Christendom presented just such a hostile environment to esoteric activity in Europe for many centuries. And there have been many other societies of this kind, religious or secular, throughout history. If it is accepted that an inner school could be engaged upon work of importance to humanity and perhaps beyond, it is obvious that it may be obliged to protect itself in this way—for the good of us all!

Secondly, certain knowledge possessed by the esoteric schools may have to be kept secret by its members from outsiders for the simple reason that it could be wrongly or dangerously used if it was acquired by the wrong people with a wrong motive. Such misuse of the school's knowledge could also interfere with the work of the school itself, which is always a highly sensitive operation.

But, it may well be asked, in view of what has already been said, how could this be possible? How, in fact, could any such danger exist if esoteric knowledge is inner knowledge accessible only to those with the concomitant inner development, as suggested earlier?

The answer is that at the outer edge of esotericism, where the esoteric meets the exoteric, where the inner meets the outer, it *is* possible to gain access to knowledge of a certain kind emanating from the inner level, without the development necessary for its full understanding and proper use. For example, a particular technique apparently easy to learn, but whose safety depends on context and control. In other words, it may be necessary to keep something secret, which though superficially accessible to ordinary consciousness, is nevertheless something that essentially belongs to, and can only be responsibly and appropriately employed by, beings of superior spiritual intelligence, who know exactly what they are doing. They know the whole of which it is a part. They are its originators. It is their private property—and rightly so. 'A little knowledge can be a dangerous thing.'

And finally, why *should* the pearl be thrown in the market place? It must surely be obvious that only those who truly seek it are worthy of finding the path to Truth. This effort is, as it always has been, a minimum requirement. 'Seek and ye shall find. Knock, and it shall be opened unto you.' says the adept, Jesus. Conversely, do not seek and ye shall not find. Don't trouble to knock—and it shall not be opened!

On this subject the Sufi master Yusuf Hamadani makes the following statement:

> The superior experience and knowledge will be made available to a man or woman in exact accordance with his or her worth, capacity and earning of it.
>
> Our objective is to achieve, by the understanding of the Origin, the Knowledge which comes through experience.

This is done, as with a journey, only with those who already know the Way.

The justice of this state is the greatest justice of all: because, while this knowledge cannot be withheld from him who deserves it, it cannot be given to him who does not deserve it.

It is the only substance with a discriminating faculty of its own, *inherent* justice.

Hamadani (1048 – 1140)

CHAPTER FIVE

The inner circle of humanity

It is clear that esotericism implies and requires the existence of higher human beings, an esoteric community, a guiding inner circle of humanity who produce, direct and sustain the education of the race. The inner teaching requires inner teachers. With them it is organically connected. For such knowledge depends on *being*, higher being, for its very existence. It is thus *being*-knowledge. It originates with, and is sustained by, beings of a certain nature, who project it downwards through a descending sequence of other beings until it reaches the recipient level of ordinary humanity. This is Jacob's Ladder. From the inner community comes the inner help by which we can ascend it. The way is indeed a *living* way. And cannot be otherwise.

The necessity for such help from intermediaries between man and God in the spiritual ascent from Earth to Heaven is well expressed by René Daumal, the narrator of the extraordinary expedition which attempted the climb of that Mountain of mountains 'whose solitary summit reaches the sphere of eternity, yet whose base spreads out

25

in manifold foothills into the world of mortals'—the colossal Mount Analogue*:

> Now, like you, in my reading and my travels, I had heard about a superior type of man, possessing the keys to everything which is a mystery to us. This idea of a higher and unknown strain within the human race was not something I could take simply as an allegory. Experience has proved, I told myself, that a man cannot reach truth directly, nor all by himself. An *intermediary* has to be present, a force still human in certain respects, yet transcending humanity in others. Somewhere on our Earth this superior form of humanity must exist, and not utterly out of reach. In that case, shouldn't all my efforts be directed towards discovering it? Apart from this hope, all life lacked meaning for me.

These are the Mountain Guides, whose help in the climb is essential. Help which depends on the very being of the helper. Which is what one of the Guides meant when he said, 'I am the Way'. And when the Sufis say, 'The teacher, the teaching and taught are one phenomenon', they are referring to this truth, and more.

Though most people are unable to accept the possible existence and activity of a higher kind of human being on the planet, unknown on the whole to ordinary mankind, there are nevertheless hints throughout history of such a presence. In all the great cultures one can discern indications of a deeper humanity, hidden like leaven within the humanity we imagine we know. The very concepts of Masters, Initiates and Adepts are evidence of this.

According to Gurdjieff, who appears to have made definite contact with beings of this order, 'The humanity to which we belong, namely the whole of historic humanity known to civilisation in reality consist of only the outer circle of humanity within which there is another inner circle.' Responsibility for the evolution of humanity, he explained, was vested in this group. Evolution meant 'the evolution of human consciousness'. He further added, 'the evolution of humanity can only proceed through the evolution of a certain group, which in its turn, will influence and lead the rest of humanity.' And, he asserted: 'The life of humanity to which we belong is governed more

---

*'Mount Analogue' René Daumal.

than we know by influences proceeding from the inner circle of humanity whose existence and significance the vast majority of people do not suspect any more than they suspect planetary influences.' Ouspensky put it like this:

> If the existence of hidden knowledge is admitted, it is admitted as belonging to certain people, but to people we do not know, to an inner circle of humanity.
>
> According to this idea, humanity is regarded as two concentric circles. All humanity which we know and to which we belong form the outer circle. All the history of humanity that we know is the history of the outer circle. But within this circle is another, of which men of the outer circle know nothing, and the existence of which they only sometimes dimly suspect— although the life of the outer circle in its most important manifestation, and particularly in its evolution, is actually guided by the inner circle. The inner or the esoteric circle forms, as it were, a life within life, a mystery, a secret in the life of humanity.
>
> The outer or esoteric humanity to which we belong is like the leaves on a tree that change every year. In spite of this they consider themselves the centre of life, not understanding that the tree has a trunk and roots, and that besides leaves, it bears flowers and fruit. The esoteric circle is, as it were, humanity *within* humanity … the immortal soul of humanity.

Ouspensky's image powerfully expresses this important and exciting. truth. Yet we know that 'ordinary' humanity too has its own flowers and fruits. In a loving relationship or a lyrical poem, in a beautiful painting or a compassionate act, in a splendid symphony or a Gershwin song, we sublunar beings too send forth our flowers from time unto eternity! 'What harmonies of earth are heard in heaven?' suggests Siegfried Sassoon.

But, returning to our theme, it might indeed well be asked, 'If these higher humans exist, where are they, and why cannot we make contact with them?'

Taking the second question first, it seems that those who truly seek their help have indeed been able to make such contact through the centuries. 'Seek and *you* shall be found.' say the Sufis. Apart from individuals for whom this contact was a private matter, which is very likely to have occurred from time to time, it is evident that the founders of all genuine developmental schools throughout history would have had contact, probably of a continuing kind, with members of the inner circle of humanity. Their help and direction would have been essential in such projects. The founders of religions, which are in reality the external aspects of internal, esoteric groups, can all be seen to have had such connection.

Zoroaster received his esoteric education at ancient Balkh in Afghanistan, a city known for its wise men and as a spiritual centre for over two thousand years. Moses was taught by initiates in Egypt. Mohammed is known to have received periodic visits by people he called 'The Rudder'—again from Afghanistan. And what does the legend of the Three Wise Men represent in the mission of Jesus? It would appear to be recognition by, and contact with, the permanent People of the Tradition, one of whose agents he undoubtedly was.

Gurdjieff, who clearly seems to have made contact with a major esoteric Centre, tells us that he ultimately found the teaching he had long sought in the monastery of the Sarmouni hidden in the highlands of the Hindu Kush. According to material acquired by Idries Shah, this is a very ancient and special community of Sufis, and it is significant that he himself has had access to such material. The powerful 'Parable of the Three Domains' made available to us by him in his 'Tales of the Dervishes' is from this source. Shah is himself a Hindu Kush Sayed, and a member of the ancient and noble family known in the East and Middle East as 'The People of the House'. Many of the great Sufi teachers over the last thousand years appear to have come from this family.

Ernest Scott, who has done much research in this field, is convinced that the Custodians of the Inner Tradition are a certain group of Sufis known as the Khwajagan, or the Order of the Masters. In his remarkable work *'The People of the Secret'* he concludes:

> Tradition asserts that for the thousands of years there has been an 'Inner Circle of Humanity' capable of thinking in terms of millennia and possessing knowledge and powers of a high order. Its members intervene from time to time in human affairs. They do this not as leaders of mankind, but unobtrusively by introducing certain ideas and techniques. This intervention works in such a way as to rectify deviations from the predicted course of human history.

Ernest Scott adds that also according to tradition, '... there is an inner circle within the Sufic membership which preserves the most vital secrets of the techniques of inner development and also the secrets of the most effective methods of manipulating environment for developmental purposes. This tradition is called the Khwajagan (Persian: 'Masters')'.

He is inclined to the view that while there may be several Centres on Earth from which such people operate, one Centre is in Afghanistan and 'corresponds to the legend of the Markaz or 'Powerhouse.'

Scott is convinced that at certain times in the history of mankind significant opportunities for such development occur which are used by the inner circle in corresponding operations. Interestingly, he observes, 'There are indications that an 'Occasion' is currently developing and that its possibilities are being focused chiefly in the West.'

Thus do the Inner People operate their Tradition, working according to the 'times'. As one of their number told Rafael Lefort, the traveller, in an unusual encounter in Tabriz in 1965, 'From the beginning of time our people have spoken the language of the people and have moved according to the time state of the planet. We are abreast of time and even ahead of it ... We are men of every century including the twenty-first.'

When Lefort asked the purpose of certain power houses in the Hindu Kush, he was informed, 'The people in those centres are concerned with the destiny of the world, but you, you cannot even begin to comprehend anything of their activities. They are no ordinary men, let alone monks. They know neither of rest nor satisfaction, for they have to make up for the shortcomings of humanity. Can you comprehend for one instant the immensity of the burden, waking and sleeping? The magnitude of the burden they carry for you?'

We cannot. Nor will we have the vaguest conception of it—until we become like them.

For these are they of the inner kingdom, breathing the inner air. Who we know not, yet who well know us. These are they who have overcome, who have ascended the Mountain, who beckon from Beyond, and draw us to our Destiny. These are the real people, the Realty, who ceaselessly sustain and uphold us from within though we know it not. Working night and day for the world—these are the true Friends of Man.

CHAPTER SIX

The way

It is clear from what has been said that 'the way' and the esoteric community who create and administer it are fused, organically connected—in some sense one. From them does it emanate, through them does it exist. For the way is a way of being, through being, to being. This is a subtle concept, without which the essential nature of the way cannot be understood. We are talking about nothing less than the transmission of very being, from higher to lower, teacher to pupil—a constant flow of being and becoming. It is literally a living way.

The term which the Sufis use for the way expresses this very well. This is 'tariqa-sufiyya' meaning 'the way of being a Sufi', or Sufi-ism. There can be no Sufism without Sufis. Wisdom is a living essence in the living wise. And 'tariqa' means both 'path'—the way that is travelled, followed; and also the way in the sense of 'method'. It is relevant to recall that the original pupils of Jesus always referred to their teaching as 'the way'. It was not until AD 45 that the term 'Christian' was first produced (Acts 11:26), and 'Christianity' very much later.

'Is a way necessary?' it is often asked. 'Cannot I find my own way?' The answer is implicit in everything that has been said.

31

And anyone who asks such questions betrays ignorance of the whole nature of the enterprise. We are talking about ascending from our present level of being and consciousness, of which we know far less than we suppose, to a higher level of being and consciousness of which we know almost nothing. Such a colossal objective, the transformation of ourselves to a different and higher kind of human being, must obviously require help, very sophisticated and powerful help, from beings above our own level, superior beings, who know us, know where we should go, and how we can get there.

'There are no ways outside the Way,' is a dictum of esotericism. By this is meant that only by means of an authentic developmental path can any raising of man's being be achieved. All else is ignorance—often taking the form of arrogance. Those, and there are many, who blithely announce that they are following their 'own path' are actually in the position of a blind man who attempts to climb a steep and difficult mountain, having, as a plains dweller all his life, no idea at all of what a 'mountain' is. One can but politely wish them very good luck!

In this connection, when Jesus said, 'Enter ye in at the strait gate: for wide is the gate, and broad is the road, that leadeth to perdition, and many there be that go in thereat: But strait is the gate, and narrow is the way that leadeth unto life, and few there be that find it.' (Matthew 7:13) he meant just that.

Two thousand years later, Gurdjieff echoes and reaffirms the statement of the earlier master. 'The ways are narrow and strait. But only by them can anything be attained. In order to grasp the essence of this teaching it is necessary very clearly to understand the idea that the ways are the *only* possible methods for the development of man's hidden possibilities.'

It is obvious that faith by itself is not enough to take you there. Nor is intuition, however wonderful and valuable it is. It is undoubtedly related to that deeper and greater intelligence we must seek. But it is only a fragment of a deeper Whole. A spark from the fire of Wisdom. It has to be developed into what Sufis sometimes call 'deep intuition', but more usually 'Perception'.

We repeat: There are no ways outside the Way. Beyond lies only the wilderness, however disguised, in which man, moving for the most part in miasmas of meaninglessness, ceaselessly somnambulating through circles of recurrent reincarnations, will remain forever lost. So find again the Ancient Way, O wanderer in time, and become a traveller to Eternity. Come, take the High Road, O dweller of the lowlands, to the Assembly of Man!

We will now attempt to 'describe', for only by actually following them could and can they be ultimately understood, a number of esoteric paths which men and women have entered and trodden in that small portion of human history that we *imagine* we know. For the real history of our race is its inner history, an invisible process which may or may not leave visible traces, and even these may not be recognised for what they really are.

Why should it be valuable to do this? And what in particular is the point of acquainting ourselves with knowledge of certain ways which though once fully alive, may no longer be organically operative?

It is submitted that a study of these ways has an enlivening and beneficial effect on the consciousness. Mysteriously, emanations still emerge from them. They are somehow invested with a timeless shining. We can even now receive something of their original radiance.

And not only is it valuable to know something of each individual path in itself, instilling into the consciousness its intrinsic insights and resonating with its own especial symbols, but also an initial period of exposure to a variety of such teachings produces a whole, a total impact. Studied in this way there occurs a cumulative effect on the consciousness as their many reverberations merge into a larger harmony. One senses simultaneously their concurrence and convergence, and receives a definite impression of persistent pattern and purpose. One becomes gradually and increasingly aware of a Way of ways, a Path of paths, discernible though and behind them all. Which, springing from an eternal Source, is ever alive. The Tree of which they are all branches.

CHAPTER SEVEN

The mystery schools

A t the heart of many an ancient culture, in its most mysterious centre, was the Mystery Cult. This was its hidden house of power whose rays influenced and infused its art and thought, informing and shaping the surrounding cultural environment in ways unknown and unseen by the vast majority of its own inhabitants, and even less suspected by the remote researcher of today.

It is clear that for ancient Greece, the Mysteries of Eleusis long performed this role. Many of its leading figures, including Socrates and Plato, admitted their initiation at, and thus connection with, this school. Having discussed the variety of expressions of Greek creativity in art, architecture, music and philosophy in his extraordinary work *'The Theory of Celestial Influence'* the thinker Rodney Collin observes, 'Yet behind this diversity we sense one informing source, some hidden centre of vitality which is suggested but never revealed by the strange role of the Eleusinian Mysteries ...'. While the esoteric historian Ernest Scott concludes, 'It is not the divergence of the Greek schools that is remarkable, but the overlap of their insights.'

But in addition to the Eleusinean Mysteries there were a number of other Mystery Schools ranged like a chain of hidden fires secretly burning across the breadth of the ancient world. There were the Orphic Mysteries, the Phrygian Mysteries, the Mysteries of Samothrace, the Chaldean and Assyrian Mysteries, and the Mysteries of Mithras, whose centres spread from their origin in Persia to Babylonia, Greece and Rome. But the oldest and probably the parent school of them all was the Egyptian Mystery Cult of Isis, and there was a tradition that the centre at Eleusis was founded by a group of Egyptian priestesses, the legendary Danaii, who were initiates of the Temple of Isis.

It appears that there was communication and mutual understanding between the mystery schools of different cultures. They knew that they were all engaged in essentially the same activity, and recognised their inner identity. Their common purpose was to provide, for those who truly sought it, access to a certain kind of esoteric education leading, through an ascending sequence of initiations, to the higher stages of consciousness possible for man. They shone across the ancient world, a constellation of centres for the cultivation of consciousness, offering ways of raising one's being to those adventurers of the heart seeking a level of life beyond the dimensions of ordinary existence.

The common aim of the mystery cults was that transformation of being which they called 'rebirth' or 'resurrection', a state in which he or she who followed the initiatory path could ultimately be 'reborn' into a higher kind of life connected in some organic way with what could be called the 'divine'. Thus it was said of the Orphic Mysteries, 'the aim was union with the divine not merely as an ecstatic experience but as the acquisition of a permanent state of being.' On a golden tablet of Orphic origin, which has been found in South Italy, are the words, 'I have flown out of the weary wheel.' indicating that the initiate has obtained release from the relentless cycle or 'wheel' of repeated incarnations. Or as the Indian mystics would say, he or she has achieved 'mokhsa', literally 'release', from the wandering circles of 'samsara'. A Mithraic papyrus discovered in Egypt refers to the spiritual rebirth necessary:

> O Lord, I have been born again
> And pass away in exaltation.
> In exaltation I die.
> Birth that produces life brings me into being

And frees me for death.
I go my way as Thou hast ordered.

In the text known as 'The Liturgy of Mithras' we read:

Today I have been born again by Thee
Out of all the myriads
For the life-giving rebirth.

Mithraists called this stage of their way 'The Sacrament', involving the 'death' of the seeker from which he would 'arise again' as a 'new man'. We are, of course, irresistibly reminded of the concepts of 'resurrection' and 'rebirth' in original Christianity, and the necessity, repeatedly emphasised, of some kind of spiritual change or transformation to take place before one could 'enter the Kingdom of Heaven'. In the words of Jesus (John 3:3), 'Verily, verily I say unto thee, Except a man be born again he cannot see the kingdom of God.' That this rebirth involved a special spiritual transformation he makes clear in the same context (John 3:5), 'Except a man be born of water, and of the spirit, he cannot enter the kingdom of God.' So therefore, 'Marvel not that I said unto thee, ye must be born again.'

In view of such consonances, it is not surprising to learn that contemporary Mystery Schools regarded the 'Christian Mysteries' as of their kind. They recognised Jesus and his pupils as being engaged in essentially the same activity as themselves—the development of human being and consciousness.

We know that at Eleusis there were three levels or stages of initiation possible. The first was called 'katharsis', meaning purification. The second 'telete', meaning initiation, and the last and highest stage or state was 'epopteia' or vision. It is therefore significant that Clement of Alexandria, teacher of a school of esoteric Christianity in that city towards the end of the second century, who claimed to be the recipient of an inner tradition of teaching from the Nazarene master, referred to three ascending degrees of development attainable on his path as 'Purification', 'Initiation', and finally 'Direct Vision'.

The ultimate state, according to Clement, was 'gnosis' or direct spiritual knowledge—the very term used by, and view held by the contemporary Gnostics both Christian and otherwise. In his writings, he often describes this elevated knowledge as 'mysteries', access to whose meaning is only through a process of initiatory education. Jesus too, it will be remembered, spoke of 'the *mysteries of the Kingdom of Heaven'*. Addressing his disciples he says (Mark 4:11), 'Unto you it is given to know the mysteries of the Kingdom of Heaven: but unto them that are outside all these things are done in parables …'. He here clearly states that they are the privileged recipients of a special education not available to those 'outside'. The Greek word used, 'exos', meaning literally 'outer', has an obvious and significant relationship to 'exoteric', which is being contrasted with 'esoteric', the outer with the inner.

In the Gnostic text known as *'The Books of the Saviour'* is recorded the following statement by Jesus which, like many other important sayings, has for one reason or another, been omitted from the canonical corpus:

> For this cause therefore have I brought keys of the mysteries of the kingdom of heaven; otherwise no flesh in the world will be saved. For without mysteries no-one will enter into the Light Kingdom, whether he be righteous or doer of wrong.

And in the same text he is also reported as saying to his disciples:

> Guard the mysteries for me and for the sons of my house.

It is significant to notice that for the Gnostic Christians 'baptism' itself was a 'mystery', and, according to their teachings, it was in fact necessary to experience 'The Three Baptisms'. That there was a series of three is evinced by none other than John the Baptist himself when he announces (Matthew 3:11), 'I indeed baptise you with water; but he that cometh after me shall baptise you with spirit, and with fire.'

John here identifies the three baptisms: the baptism of 'water'; the baptism of spirit or 'air'—for the Greek work 'pneuma' can be translated as either 'spirit' or 'air"; and finally the baptism of 'fire'. In esoteric developmental symbology Earth, Water, Air and Fire have always represented a succession of states of ever-increasing refinement possible to the human being, beginning with 'earth', the comparatively 'coarse' condition of ordinary planetary man, and ascending through a gradient of consciousness to the highest and subtlest state of 'fire'.

If we look again at Jesus' statement, 'Except a man be born of water, and of the spirit, he cannot enter the kingdom of God.' From this point of view, parallel with the declaration of John the Baptist, it becomes apparent that 'the kingdom of God' or the 'kingdom of heaven' is the state of 'fire'. Both John and Jesus are using the traditional symbology of mystical schools, and in particular that of ancient and medieval Alchemy, to signify the sequence of 'baptisms' or initiations required for the refinement of human consciousness. All masters of the Mysteries would have understood.

CHAPTER EIGHT

The Gnostics

During the early centuries of the Christian era, a rich and strange profusion of Gnostic societies or schools mysteriously manifested and iridescently irrupted throughout the Near and Middle East. Those which have been called Christian Gnostics, claimed to possess a secret connection with the original teachings of Jesus and regarded themselves as the inheritors of an esoteric Christian tradition unknown by, and incomprehensible to, the orthodox—as did the Valentinians, Carpocratians and Basilideans. But other schools, like the Naasenes, the Barbelites and the Ophites, indicate no obvious relationship with Christianity, and we do not know the source from which they spring. It may indeed be that their common origin was extra-historical.

The Gnostics sought 'Gnosis', which means 'knowledge'. This was not knowledge in the usual sense, but transcendental or mystical knowledge available only through spiritual illumination arrived at as a result of special effort and education. One would then become a 'Knower', possessed of a permanent state of knowing, a higher level of perception, and thus be able to fully and consciously participate in the Life of the Universe. This was the Gnostic quest.

41

But regretfully, the 'normal' condition of man, according to the Gnostic, is one of ignorant sleep or 'agnoia', a state into which man has fallen unconscious of his identity, origin and destiny. He has become hypnotised by the world and suffers from a kind of amnesia. Oblivious of his origin, forgetful of his mission, he wanders wanly sleepwalking through the 'Kenoma'—the 'Land of Lack'. He lacks memory, consciousness, purpose; and thus, of course, fulfilment. As the Gnostic teacher, Valentinus, tells us in his work '*The Gospel of Truth*', recently recovered from the sands of Egypt, 'He who is a-gnostic lacks, and indeed it is a great thing that he lacks. It is that which would complete him.'

'Completion' therefore is the Gnostic aim. It is also that of the Sufis who say, 'Mankind is asleep in a nightmare of unfulfilment. He must awaken, to become Insan-i-Kamil, the Complete Man.' For only the complete can completely play his complete part in the Universe. Only the real can really inhabit reality. 'Unless a man is born from above he cannot enter the Kingdom.'

Deep above us, say the Gnostics is the Pleroma or Place of Fullness where the sons and daughters of God flower. This is the Realm of Reality where the aspirant can attain 'the Reunion'. According to Gnostic teaching this is a state in which one is reunited with one's real self and with God. 'In the Reunion each one shall receive *himself*.' says Valentinus. Which statement reminds us of the words of an ancient sage, 'I have come out of all things unto myself.' And we also recall the story of a certain prodigal who 'having journeyed into a far country, and there wasted his *substance*' finally 'came to himself',* and returned to his father (Luke 15).

'The Return' is a central concept of the Gnostics, who quote Jesus as having said, 'Seek, and ye shall receive a return.' Valentinus explains 'this return is called change of consciousness'—a statement clearly indicating the nature of their activity. While in The Gospel of Truth we are told:

---

*This quotation from the parable of the Prodigal Son is, of course, from the Authorised Version of the New Testament (1611), most of whose poetry, power and meaning springs directly from the poet Tyndale's inspired translation of 1526. Interestingly, instead of 'came to himself' in the later version, Tyndale's translation is 'Then he remembered hymsilfe… .'

The Father, who withholds within Himself their completeness
gives it to them as a return to Himself and a Gnosis, which is
Perfection.

Gnosis is perfection. But man as he is, as he finds himself in his ordinary state, is imperfect. His task, his work, is to perfect himself, say
the Gnostics. Then he enters into his 'Inheritance'—the higher state of
illumination and power that is his true potential. This self-realisation
was the aim of the Gnostic schools. The Naasenes described it as
'attaining your true nature'. And, more recently, Maurice Nicoll as
'achieving one's *inner* destiny.'
   In the words of the Gospel of Truth:

> I have been like the shadows and fantasies of the night.
> But now I leave them behind like a dream
> And awaken to the Gnosis of the Father.

Thus doth the seeker arise form his sleep and return to Reality.
He has reached the Pleroma, where the Peacock of Possibility out-
spreads wide its feathers. Where I am *really* I, and you are really *you*.
And the dreams you never dreamed of do come true!

Know yourself

The Gnostic teacher, Theodotus, successor of Valentinus, states, as
quoted by Clement of Alexandria in his 'Excerpts from Theodotus,
'He who has attained the Gnosis is able to know: Who we are? What
we have become? Where we have been cast? From what we must
be freed? Where we are to go? What birth is? And what rebirth is?'
Theodotus contrasts such knowledge with the normal human condition of 'aporeia'—'roadlessness' or 'not knowing where one is going'.
   It can be seen from the first question Theodotus asks that an
essential element in the Gnostic endeavour was to 'know yourself'.
What 'knowing yourself' really means is a difficult concept—only
to be fully understood through the actual achievement *of* knowing yourself. One can of course say that it is an enlightened state of
self-knowledge. This would mean knowledge of the nature of one's
true or inner self, a realisation of one's real identity. And this would
require knowledge of the outer, or as the Sufis describe it, 'second-
ary' self, and the manner in which it holds the inner self in bondage.

The nature of human bondage was in fact of central interest to the Gnostics and a special object of their study. Their constant theme was that man is in 'prison' in this sublunar realm, and that the process of escape was a skilled activity in which outside help was essential. This the Gnostic teacher would provide. Knowledge of one's self was thus both a means and an end of the escape operation.

The Gnostic literature discovered in December 1945, in a large earthenware jar buried under the sands of Egypt near the town of Nag Hammadi, where it had lain hidden for one thousand six hundred years, abounds with the exhortation 'know yourself'. It does not of course tell us *how* to do this—a matter only to be understood through full involvement in a Gnostic school with its teacher and techniques. This literature, as that of any true developmental entity, must always be seen in such a context. It is part of a larger, organic, operational whole.

Thus in the text entitled *'Teachings of Silvanus'*, the student is told, 'Before everything, know yourself.' In *'Allogenes'* ('The Stranger') we read, 'O Allogenes, behold your blessedness ... in silence wherein you know yourself as you are, and, seeking, yourself ascend to the Life.'

In 'The Book of Thomas the Contender' Jesus is quoted as saying tersely, 'Whoever has not known himself has known nothing.' While in the Gospel of Thomas he tells us:

> The Kingdom is within you and without you.
> If you know yourselves then you will be known, and you will know you are the Sons and Daughters of the Father.
> But if you do not know yourselves, then
> You are in poverty, and you are poverty.

With such instruction, the Nazarene teacher is clearly placing himself not only in the company of the Gnostics, but also very firmly in the direct line of the ancient Wisdom Tradition of which he is the representative and transmitter. Six hundred years before him the Chinese sage Lao-Tzu had said, 'He who knows himself is enlightened.' (Tao-te Ching). While the inscription above the entrance to the Oracle at Delphi, words attributed to the Greek philosopher Thales of Miletus (about 590 BC) read, as it still reads, 'Gnothi Seauton'—'Know Thyself'.

It is sad indeed that the four familiar Gospels are bereft and deprived of such important material. Orthodox Christianity or 'Churchianity' as it has been more accurately termed, had, and has, no conception whatsoever of this matter. Through a compound of ignorance and arrogance, it entirely excluded itself and its adherents from this and other essential aspects of the Master's teachings. And the curious doctrines it has instead produced have ensured its continued stultification and paralysis. Morality is mistaken for spirituality. Doctrine replaces development.

But unknown to the externalists, and beyond their understanding, the inner stream of real teaching flowed on.

The universe of the Gnostics

The Gnostics believed—they would say *knew*—that the great Universe, visible and invisible, was created by a Supreme Being— God, who is Alone, Ineffable, Beyond, Above, and yet mysteriously Within, all His Creation. Not only did He create, but He continually sustains, everything. In this sense His creation is a continual and continuous activity. Unless He upheld it—all would cease to exist. 'From the invisible springs the visible.' said the mediaeval mystic John Scot Eringena, who understood such matters.

To quote a Gnostic prayer:

> Thou alone art the Boundless, the uncontainable,
> The unshakeable, and the Unknowable.
> Thou art Love and Source of All.
> Hear me in sooth, Father imperishable,
> Immortal, God of the hidden worlds,
> Thou only Light and Life.

Somewhat later, in sixteenth century England, Joshua Sylvester wrote a poem which the Gnostics would have liked:

The Father

> Alpha and Omega, God Alone:
> Eloi, My God, the Holy One,
> Whose Power is Omnipotence,
> Whose Wisedom is Omniscience,
> Whose Being is All Soveraigne Blisse,
> Whose Worke Perfection's Fulnesse is:
> Under All things, not under-cast;
> Over All things, not over-plac't.

Within All things, not there included;
Without All things, not thence excluded.
Above All, over All things raigning,
Beneath All, All things aye sustaining;

Without All, All conteyning sole:
Within All, filling-full the Whole;
Within All, no where comprehended;
Without All, no where more extended.

Today, Tomorrow, Yesterday,
With Thee are One, and instant aye;
Aye undivided, ended never,
Today, with Thee, indures forever.

Thow wert, Thou art, Thou wilt be ever;
And thine Elect, rejecteth never.

From on High this Most Mysterious Being creates in a downward flow of emanation an ever-descending succession of worlds or levels of being, each emerging from the one above and within it, in a cascading gradient of consciousness and life, from the finest of the fine to the most material at the lowest end of the spectrum.

The world closest to the Creator was called by the Gnostics the 'Light Kingdom' or 'Kingdom of Light', wherein dwelt beings of the very highest subtlety of consciousness. Below this realm was a descending sequence of 'Aeons' or planes of being and intelligence in the downward Chain of worlds.

Humanity occupied a world or level four stages above the lowest, and just below 'The Lower Firmament'. This was, however, not the true and 'rightful' domain of the human soul or 'pneuma', which in some way had fallen from a very much higher realm into a world where it did not really belong. Man was thus a 'stranger' ('allogenes') here. His origin was elsewhere, and to it he must return.

And so in the Gospel of Thomas:

Jesus said, 'Blessed are the solitary and elect,
For you shall find the Kingdom;
Because you came from it,
And you shall go there again.
And if they say to you

'From where have you originated?'
Say to them,
'We have come from the Light.'

Gnostic concept of 'The Fall'

The Gnostic view of the 'Fall of Man' had nothing whatsoever to do with moral fault. It was entirely a fall in *perception*, a lowering of consciousness. The Gnostics would have shared William Blake's image of 'encaverned man ... enclosed in his senses five', which was very similar to their own concept of man 'in prison' here below.

According to the Gnostics, the essential, inner or 'light-being' of man originated in the Light World, or, as they often called it, 'The Treasury of Light'. Yet this being was a 'seed' rather than a flower. It had to grow, it had to become. So a descent to a 'growing medium', this world, was necessary. There it would be buried, break through the surface of things, and blossom[†].

From the high world of Light the soul was lowered. Down, down, down through Aeon after Aeon it descended, until at last it reached this planet or plane, this vale of Forgetting, where it forgot, or only dimly remembered, its high Origin, the Light Kingdom from which it had been exiled.

Very appropriately, the Gnostics categorised human beings according to the degree of their forgetfulness, or conversely, of their memory, of their source. The range was from total amnesia, through vague recollection, to full memory and awareness of origin. The latter would only be those who had realised the Gnosis. The rest of mankind, using this criterion, they 'classified' as of two kinds: the 'choic' or 'earthbound' men, who constituted the vast majority, thoroughly asleep, utterly hypnotised by the 'Archon' of this world, a being whose aim it was to keep mankind in this somnolent state, and prevent its evolution; and the 'psychic', using this word in their own special sense, to represent the portion of humanity, regretfully not large, who still had some dim remembrance

---

[†]We are reminded of Jesus' words: 'Except a corn of wheat fall into the ground and die, it abideth alone; but if it die, it bringeth forth much fruit.' (John 12:24)

of their origins, some faint flickering sense of exile, some vague suspicion that they had lost contact with a Destiny that lay somewhere beyond and above an environment that pressed and preyed upon them from all sides—posturing as the only world there was, the only place of being, the only reality. These were the ones with possibility, with the potentiality that could be liberated from its 'prison', and developed, whose inner ears could hear the Gnostic call to awaken: 'I am the Voice of Awakening in the Night'—and who would answer it.

The Gnostic survival

Did Gnosticism disappear as a result of the continued and ever-increasing opposition and persecution by the established Church? The answer must surely be no. It is impossible to believe that a movement of such power and profundity, vision and vitality, could ever be essentially suppressed. The inner stream would flow on, hidden, to emerge in perhaps another form, at another time, in another place. Its Source would ensure that.

Inevitably, however, faced by the uncomprehending hostility of that particular persuasion of Christianity, which called itself the Church, in those times merely one sect among many, but whose strength increased in no relation to its spirituality, until by acquiring the support of the Roman state it found itself in a dominating position, the Gnostic Christians were compelled to 'leave the scene'.

The Gnostic societies undoubtedly constituted a very serious challenge to the authority that this sect, the orthodox Church, had assumed, and a major threat to its identity and self-image. The Gnostic claim, explicit as much as implicit, to be the real spiritual hierarchy, was a danger that could not be ignored. One can but sympathise. It is not particularly pleasant to be called 'unknowingly empty', or 'dry waterless canals', for those who regard themselves as Christ's representatives, nor can it be taken as complimentary to be informed that their organisation is only a 'counterfeit'!

It was not surprising, therefore, though they were not ready to do this till the end of the second century, that the leaders of the Church declared the Gnostic groups 'heretics'. They themselves, however, did not accept the accuracy of this designation, preferring the term 'esotericists'.

But, as was to be expected, the Churchians proceeded to seek out and burn any Gnostic text they could lay their hands on, while Irenaeus, bishop of Lyon, remote both in distance and in intelligence from Gnostic activity, produced a series of distraught and distorted diatribes against 'the heretics' form his lair in France!

The situation became worse when in 313 AD the Roman emperor Constantine proclaimed himself a Christian, for now the Church's policy had state support. Not only were many more of their books burnt, but from then on the 'heretics' found their very lives at risk. Under the Emperor Theodosius in the 380's, persecution increased.

The Gnostics were thus obliged at first to adopt a low profile—and finally forced to go underground. It is likely that it was about this time that the collection of Gnostic texts known today as the Nag Hammadi Library was buried in a tall jar in the Egyptian sands near the ancient town of Chenoboskion.

Thus it was that the Gnostics disappeared from what is usually regarded as 'history'; or, more accurately, disappeared from view. The current continued to flow, covertly; the stream still sought the sea—but from now on through a subterranean channel. Occasionally it emerged to the surface, suddenly flashing into the sun.

One such appearance was in the form of the powerful movement known as Catharism, or as the Churchmen called it, 'The Albigensian Heresy'—because its main centre was at Albi in Southern France. It mysteriously arrived in Western Europe 'from the East' about the middle of the twelfth century, rapidly influencing a number of cultured men and women as well as many ordinary people who could not be satisfied with the Catholic view of things. The Cathars produced a thorough and widespread organisation, which constituted such a threat to the orthodox version of Christianity that the Church was unable to tolerate its continued existence. The subsequent persecution of the Cathars was so relentless that few traces of their ideas and doctrines remained.

That Catharism was connected to Gnosticism is generally accepted by the scholars and experts in the field. Benjamin Walker, in his study entitled 'Gnosticism', informs us that 'Cathars', meaning 'the pure ones' was the name assumed by, or given to, a number of heretical Christian sects that flourished between the third and eleventh centuries in Armenia, Syria and Asia Minor, and from there spread to Western Europe. He is convinced of an influence 'stemming form Gnosticism'. Ernest Scott, the remarkable researcher into esoteric intervention in history, states, 'Catharism came from the East and was apparently rooted in Gnosticism.'

As Cathar means 'a pure one', it is obvious that a certain kind of purification was involved. It appears that they practiced a form of baptism called the 'consolamentum', in which 'one's own spirit was brought into contact with a higher and greater spirit'. We are clearly talking about an initiatory process.

The Gnostics today

Whether or not Catharism was a form of Gnosticism—and perhaps we lack the information to be totally sure—is there any evidence to suggest the continued existence of Gnostic schools today? Arkon Daraul, traveller and authority on present and past esoteric and occult organisations, reports as follows in his work 'Secret Societies':

> In more than one place in the Middle East, as well as in small groups in Western Europe, there are still followers of various schools of Gnosticisms. They mainly follow the ideas held by Valentinus, with some variations.... Little or no investigation of these 'People of Wisdom' has been done by research workers on the spot—in Asia and North Africa—where strong and interesting traces of their beliefs and practices still remain.

As a result of his contact with, and study of, contemporary Gnostic societies, Daraul concludes:

> The main teaching states that there is a Supreme Being or Power which is invisible and has no perceptible form. This Power can be contacted by mankind, and it is through it that man can control himself and work out his destiny. The various teachers through the ages, putting their creeds in many different ways, were in contact with this Power, and their religions all contain a more or less hidden kernel of initiation. This is the secret which the Knowers can communicate to their disciples. Bu the secret can be acquired only through exercising the mind and the body, until the terrestrial man is so refined as to be able to become a vehicle for the use

of this Power. Eventually the initiate becomes identified with the Power, and in the end attains his true identity as a purified personality, infinitely superior to the rest of unenlightened mankind.

Daraul is here generalising to some extent beyond his actual observations of the Gnostic schools. But it is doubtless a conclusion he has come to as a result of his prolonged study of esoteric activity of various kinds. And one with which the present writer fully concurs. Daraul then continues:

> The symbolism in which this teaching is concealed, the methods by which the mystical power is attained, vary from one Gnostic society to another. But the constant factor is there: the attainment of that which humankind unconsciously needs.

He explains that according to the Gnostics there is in every man and woman a certain sense of unfulfilment, and that 'This feeling has been put into man in order that he may seek the fulfilment that the Gnostics can give him.'

Daraul is clearly convinced of the authenticity of the Gnostic activity he has encountered. But he stresses that it cannot be understood by a reading of their literature alone, which must, he says, be accompanied by 'the rituals and practices which are used to produce the Gnosis, the enlightenment.' The literature is thus 'operational', part of a larger, deeper process, and only truly accessible and meaningful when approached and received in the actual teaching context of a living Gnostic school. This concurs with the view I have expressed earlier of the nature of the Nag Hammadi texts. And interestingly, this is also exactly the role of Sufi literature according to authentic exponents of the Sufi path.

There are in fact similarities between Gnosticism and Sufism, which are impossible to ignore. Both have as their objective, Knowledge. The Sufi term 'marifat' can be literally translated as 'gnosis' or experiential knowledge. Again, the Sufi Adept is known as an 'Arif', which the contemporary master Omar Ali Shah translates as 'Gnostic or person who has gnosis or direct knowledge of Divine Reality'.

In his book, Arkon Daraul gives us an interesting illustration, which tends to indicate that the essence of Gnosticism is now to be contacted, subsumed, within the Sufi current.

Altar of a Western secret socicty with Sufi
and Gnostic affinities. The knot-motif symbolises
the 'Great Secret' of the Society.

CHAPTER NINE

The art of alchemy

'Aurum nostrum non est aurum vulgare', claimed the Alchemists—'Our gold is not common gold.' So if the Alchemists of the Middle Ages were not, as is usually assumed, concerned with the production of ordinary gold from base metals like lead or iron, what kind of gold *did* they seek to make?

The answer is bright and shining inner gold, the gold from which souls are made, no less—'sophic' gold, as they called it. From heavy, leaden, ordinary man they sought to fashion light, golden, spiritual man—beginning with *themselves*. For the first work of the true alchemist was to refine and transmute his own very *self* from coarse to fine, from lower to higher; and then to help others to effect the same change.

Without the guidance of the already golden man, a 'changed one', without his mastery, the transmutation could not be achieved. As a member of the alchemical fraternity told Helvetius of the Hague in 1666, 'Nay, without the communication of a true adept philosopher not one student can find the way to prepare this great magistry.' The student, too, had to be of a certain quality, 'Scarce three in one million canst be candidates for the Work of Holy Alkimy.' says Thomas Norton in his '*Ordinall of Alkimy*' (1477).

The great Persian philosopher and Sufi adept, El-Ghazali (1058–1111), known in the West as Algazel, states in his masterwork 'The Alchemy of Happiness', 'Alchemical gold is better than gold, but real alchemists are rare, and so are true Sufis.' He further tells us, '… man's happiness undergoes successive refinements according to his state of being.' In his 'Minhaj el-Abidin' he describes the progress of the alchemising of the human consciousness in 'seven valleys' of experience: the valleys of Knowledge, Turning Back, Obstacles, Tribulations, Lighting, Abysses and Praise. 'Fulfilment', he avers, 'is a property only of Paradise, entry into which depends on alchemical transmutation.'

That Ghazali uses the alchemy metaphor is not surprising, for there is a clear connection between Sufis and Alchemists through-out the Middle Ages. In fact, both he and the great twelfth century Sufi teacher, Jalaluddin Rumi, actually refer to Sufism as Alchemy from time to time in their works. It is also significant that the Golden Head, 'sar-i-tali' in Arabic, is a Sufi term referring to a person whose inner consciousness has been 'transmuted into gold' by means of Sufic study.

The connection is established beyond doubt by the fact that while the mysterious Hermes Trismegistus of ancient Egypt is tradition-ally regarded as the originator of alchemy—the Hermetic Art, the founding father of Arab European alchemy since the eighth cen-tury of the present era is always held to be Jabir Ibn el-Hayyan (721–776), called Jabir the Sufi, and known to the West as Geber. Behind him, however, stands his own teacher, the Sufi master Jafaq Sadiq (700–765) who wrote 'The Perception', an esoteric text casting much light on the inner nature of the alchemical quest.

Jabir himself was the author of over three hundred treatises on alchemy, but it was not until 1144 that Robert of Chester, who studied in Saracenic Spain, produced for the West a translation of Jabir's major text, 'The Book of the Composition of Alchemia', which first gave us the word 'alchemy'—from the Arabic 'al-kimia'. This, in turn, was derived from the old Semitic name for Egypt—'Kem'—meaning black, the distinctive colour of its alluvial soil after the flooding of the Nile, in contrast to the white sand of the surrounding desert. Alchemy was thus the Egyptian Art, or the Art of Egypt. The Arab alchemists believed themselves to be the recip-ients of the ancient teaching of Hermes through Dhu'l-Nun, the

Egyptian, known as 'Lord of the Fish' and a Sufi exponent of the highest order.

However, it is now recognised that Alchemy was practiced in all the great civilisations; and no matter whether in India, China or Greece, it was invariably called 'The Work' or 'The Great Work'. Furthermore, in whatever culture it manifested itself, there were always the same three elements: 'mercury', 'sulphur' and 'salt', which had to be combined for the production of the Philosopher's Stone. The consistency is significant. It indicates not haphazard experimentation, but a constant body of knowledge.

Alchemical terminology thus appears to be the symbolic mode of expression adopted by an esoteric developmental school for the projection of its allegorised message. It contained concealed instructions for, and description of, processes leading to the perfecting of the human being. This was technical material for the transformation of consciousness, a disguised spiritual path. 'Our gold is not your gold, and our sulphur is not your sulphur.' states the 'Rosarium Philosophorum'—the Rosary of the Philosopher—and adds, 'Only he who knows how to make the Philosopher's Stone understand the words that relate to it.' The Adept, we are reminded, is essential.

What then *is* the Philosopher's Stone, which the alchemists deemed so necessary for the making of golden men and women, and which was, it seems, the very heart of their quest? It would appear to be none other than the heart of man himself. Like the Kingdom of Heaven—it is within. Idries Shah gives us the Sufi view:

> The stone, the hidden thing, so powerful, is also called the Azoth in the West. Azoth is traced by Orientalists to the Arabic 'el-dhat' (or ez-zat), meaning essence or inner reality. The stone, according to the Sufis, is the 'dhat', the essence, which is so powerful that it can transform whatever comes into contact with it. It is the essence of man, which partakes of what peopled call the divine. It is 'sunshine' capable of uplifting humanity to a next stage.
>
> The Sophic stone is the Sufic stone.

'The stone is of exalted purity, and he who makes it makes *himself* perfect.' says the fifteenth century alchemist Thomas Norton, informing us also that it is, 'the result of concentration, distillation and refinement.' These terms refer to work on *oneself* and inner refinement—the refinement of essence. It is noteworthy that Sufis have described *their* activity as 'the refinement of the consciousness.'

The mediaeval occult philosopher, Cornelius Agrippa (born 1486), is explicit, 'The stone is *not* a stone. It is an internal spirit within us.' Of alchemy he says, 'This is the true and occult philosophy which men seek. The key thereof is the understanding. For the higher we carry our knowledge, the more sublime are our attainments in virtue, and we perform the greatest things with more ease.' Three hundred years later, the English lady alchemist, Mary Anne Atwood, was to write in her book 'A Suggestive Inquiry into the Hermetic Mystery': 'Alchemy is divine Art, the very transmutation of life itself. The spirit teaches its own Art, and according as it is obeyed the artist goes on developing the way to advance to perfection.' Agrippa and Mary Atwood may be separated by time, but not in activity.

She continues, 'Thus being awakened and at the same time drawn centrally, the consciousness comes to know and feel itself in its own true source, which is the Universal Centre and Source of all things.'

In ancient China, the Art was called 'nei-tan', inner alchemy, and was usually found interwoven with Taoism, with which it was held to esoterically correspond. Thus a later practitioner of nei-tan, Chang Po-tuan, who lived in the eleventh century, states in his *'Treatise on the Golden Elixir'*:

> Volatility transmutes into true essence;
> The human mind changes into the mind of Tao
> Without refinement by the spiritual fire
> How can gold be separated from the ore?

Enlightenment was often referred to as discovering or uncovering the inner or golden elixir; while it will be remembered that the alchemists of the West sought the mysterious Elixir of Life—doubtless another name for the Philosopher's Stone.

Both Taoists and practitioners of nei-tan describe the process of spiritual development as the fashioning of 'the sacred embryo', the 'shang-tsi', a new being that must grow and develop within; or as the growth and unfolding of 'the golden flower', whose petals only fully open upon enlightenment. Thus the alchemist Lu Tsu declares,

'I must diligently plant my own field. There is within it a spiritual seed. Its flower is like yellow gold. Its bud is not large. Its growth depends upon the soil of the central palace, but its irrigation must come from a higher fountain.'

Idries Shah interprets this as follows, 'Man must develop by his own effort, toward growth of an evolutionary nature, increasing his consciousness. He has within him an essence, initially tiny, shining, precious. Development depends upon man, but must start through a teacher.'

With regard to the need for superior help, the Viridarium Chymicum concurs: 'For the Whole Work of Philosophy the start is the Master who brings the Key.' The presence of the master is essential. Without him the work cannot be accomplished. For he acts like the Philosopher's Stone itself upon his disciples. 'The lower is transformed by contact with the higher.' Through his spiritual power he directs and nourishes his pupils. His knowledge guides, his radiance refines them. In his blessing their flowers unfold.

As one great Alchemist has said:

> The Kingdom of Heaven
> is like a grain of mustard seed,
> which a man took, and sowed in his field:
> which indeed is the least of all seeds.
> But when it is grown, it is greatest among herbs,
> and becometh a tree
> so that the birds of the air come
> And lodge in the branches thereof.
>   (Matthew 14: 31–32)

So wisdom is something that grows. It is a living thing. It is not 'acquired', like information, but absorbed. We grow in wisdom as we grow *into* wisdom. We must receive it, embrace it, become part of its very texture and allow it to become part of our very texture. For verily it is 'the Dayspring from on High that visits us.'

The occasion

It was always a law of Alchemy that the accomplishment of The Magnum Opus, The Great Work, depended on an influence beyond the alchemist's own control, called 'celestial virtue'. Little was written on the subject, but the practitioners of the art appear to have been referring to some kind of cosmic power without which the desired transmutation could not be effected. Unless the 'Solar Wind' blows, gold will not grow.

The transformation thus required a particular cosmic situation, a special Context, in which extradimensional influences were focused upon the place of work, helping to fire the 'athanor', the alchemical furnace. It is relevant that the word 'context' means literally 'woven together'.

So the timing of the alchemical operation had to be right. It had to synchronise with a higher pattern. A celestial correspondence was necessary. A certain transdimensional alignment and harmony enabled the activity to be successfully performed.

In ancient Greek thought, the term 'chronos' means time in the usual sense of 'duration', the concept of the onward stream of time, ever flowing from the future into the present and then to the past. 'Kairos' means right time, ripe time, time infused with opportunity, presenting possibility, opening outwards—beyond itself. And 'aeon' is eternity, beyond and above time—a higher dimension of the Universe.

The right time, the kairos, occurred when there was an alignment, a contact, between chronos and aeon—time and eternity. This was the alchemical opportunity, the 'Occasion', when the work could be done.

As the Alchemist of Nazareth stressed, the Work must be done 'while it is day: the night cometh when no man can work.' (John 9:4).

The fullest expression of this concept can be seen in the Sufi doctrine of 'The time, the place, and the people.' Unless, say the Sufis, a school is founded on a co-incidence of the right time, the right place, and the right people, their Teaching cannot be transmitted. In one of their tales,* which is designed to communicate this truth, it is said that certain things can only happen 'when an appropriate wave of the unseen laps upon the shore of possibility.'

---

*See 'Tales of the Dervishes' by Idries Shah—Octagon Press, 1967. The tale is 'The Time, the Place, and the People' by Sayed Imarn Ali Shah.

CHAPTER TEN

Zen

Zen. This short word with its sudden, sharp, sound conveys something of what it means. It is said to be derived from 'dhyana', Sanskrit for 'meditation', becoming 'ch'an' in China. But the Japanese expression 'Zen', which it received when it reached that culture toward the end of the twelfth century with the founding of the Rinzai School there by Eisai in 1191 AD, is infused with a peculiar implosive power and directness of trajectory—as of an arrow abruptly shot from a bowstring—which is the very essence of Zen. It well expresses the distinctive quality of the 'koan', the shock-question or question-shock technique to defeat and break through one's ordinary consciousness, which is used by the Sudden or Rinzai School.

Though Zen is often regarded as a form of Buddhism, that is certainly not the impression received when one looks openly and directly at this particular teaching. It is clearly very different from, and runs counter in every way to, the soulless and vacuous abstractionism, the arid and cumbersome pseudo-intellectuality of Buddhism as it has come to us, weighed down with its heavy edifice of doctrine and dogma.

In contrast to this petrified forest of fixed and sterile concepts, Zen is a fast and freely flowing stream, akin and similar to Taoism in its sense of flow, and in tapping the springs of spontaneity. No wonder Zen found a ready reception in Taoist China.

When Bodhidharma brought Zen from India to China in about 520 AD, he described his teaching as:

> A special transmission outside the scriptures,
> No dependence on doctrine;
> Direct pointing at the human heart,
> Seeing into one's own essence.

There we have it. Zen penetrates beyond cluttering concepts and stifling sutras to the heart beyond and within. But, while not depending on doctrine, Zen, like other spiritual traditions, does indeed depend upon the master, the teacher, who, receiving the teaching from his own master, passes it on in his turn to a successor. This is aptly called 'The Transmission of the Lamp'—as when the flame of one lamp lights the wick of another, and that another, and so on in a flowing sequence of light.

The Zen master 'incarnates' the teaching, and without him the direct transmission so essential to Zen, the 'direct pointing at the heart', cannot occur. The term 'ishin-denshin', meaning direct communication from mind to mind, describes this process of teaching-contact between master and pupil. This is the essence of the 'special transmission outside the scriptures' referred to by Bodhidharma. It takes place in the 'dokusan', the private personal interview between Zen master and pupil so important in the Rinzai school; and also in the 'mondo'—the short, rapid question and answer sequence in which the master attempts to force a response from his pupil that is immediate, that is not mediated by and thus outside his normal pattern of thinking; and also immediate in the sense of instantaneous, without time for thought as normally understood. There the two meanings fuse, when an immediate answer is demanded of an 'impossible' question. Such as, 'What is the sound of one hand clapping?'

This last, while originating in the context of a mondo, has become a koan in major use in schools of Zen. In fact, many koans are produced and derived in this way, being the essential question of the mondo interchange, extracted and used as a special concentration-exercise, a focus for prolonged attention by the student, in order to provoke a constructive implosion upon the consciousness, revealing another and deeper level of awareness. The koan is thus an impossible question, or demand, aimed at outwitting, defeating, paralysing one's ordinary thinking—to uncover, discover, expose an inner level of consciousness normally overlaid and hidden by this outer kind of thinking. It is 'impossible' only because it is not possible to 'answer' it by ordinary thinking. It is a demand that cannot be met in the normal manner. The response must arise from a different source—an inner spring of spontaneity.

When Zen came to China it met and meshed with the Taoist mystical tradition already in existence there for a thousand years. The central text of Taoism, the 'Tao Te Ching'—the Book of the Way and Its Power—has as its theme the cultivation of 'wu-wei', an inner spontaneity released in a state of openness and freedom from external control similar to the state of inner exposure, which the Zen koan is designed to produce. By 'not-thinking' a deeper intelligence is enabled to operate.

The Sufis regard Zen as a deteriorated branch of their own Teaching, which they carried to China from India in order to effect a spiritual rescue operation in that culture by making use of anything of value in Taoism and Buddhism that they found there—the standard Sufi approach.

There are without doubt similarities between Zen and Sufism that support this assertion. Like Sufism, Zen is not bound to doctrine or dogma. It is purely 'technical' and free-moving, though considerably less so than the Sufi Teaching, which throughout the centuries has projected itself successfully into a wide variety of cultures and communities. Especially clear, however, is the similarity of the koan to the 'zarb' or impact technique of the Sufis, who nevertheless maintain that it resembles only part of the totality of their technique. The Sufi 'shock' is only one element in the very wide, sophisticated and sensitive operation of the zarb technique.

A mode of teaching pertaining both to Zen and Sufi methodology is what can be called 'the presentation straight to the face', the provocation of a direct perception by the seeker—the immediate seeing of what is *before* you.

A rather intellectual Zen monk was no nearer understanding reality than he had been when he first entered the monastery five years earlier. So the master took him up to a parapet overlooking a pond. 'Look down and tell me what you see,' ordered the master. 'I see an ornamental pond, circular in shape …' began the student, but as he was speaking, the master suddenly pushed him off the parapet head first into the water below. As his face broke the surface, the monk shouted up, 'Thank you, O master, I am now enlightened!'

In reply to the question 'What is Zen?', the master Yengo (1566–1642) wrote:

> It is presented right to your face, and at this moment the whole thing is handed over to you. For an intelligent person one word should suffice to convince him of the truth of it, but even then error has crept in. The great truth of Zen is possessed by everybody. Look into your own being and seek it not elsewhere. Your own mind is above all forms. It is free and quiet. In it light is absorbed. Transcend the intellect, sever yourself from it and directly penetrate deep into the inner mind.'

We are reminded of the words of Rumi, the Sufi teacher, in his book 'The Diwan of Shams of Tabriz': 'Shut both eyes of the head, that you may see with your inner eye. Open the two arms of your self, if you seek an embrace.'

Let us now look at a story Sufis use for teaching purposes:

The smuggler

Nasrudin used to ride his donkey across the frontier time and time again with two panniers of straw. He always trudged back without them. Since he admitted to being a smuggler, the guards searched him and the straw very thoroughly each time. Meanwhile, he was visibly becoming more and more prosperous in appearance.

Eventually, years later, he went to live in another country. One of the customs men met him there. 'You can tell me now, Nasrudin. Whatever was it you were smuggling that we could never catch you?'

'Donkeys,' said Nasrudin.

Here assumptions about what they were looking for prevented the searchers form finding what was there to be found. These assumptions precluded them from seeing what was *before their very faces.* They fixed their view, and limited their field of vision. The searchers were thus locked into a particular pattern of thought that prevented their seeing straight ahead, at what was directly in front of them— 'before their very eyes'. Mankind is like this, say the Sufis, living enmeshed in an invisible net of assumptions.

The contemporary Sufi teacher, Idries Shah, makes this comment: 'Because the average person thinks in patterns and cannot accommodate himself to a really different point of view, he loses a great deal of the meaning of life. He may live, even progress, but he cannot understand all that is going on. The story of the smuggler makes this very clear.'

Shah further observes: 'The story also emphasises one of the major contentions of Sufism—that preternatural experience and the mystical goal is something nearer to man that is realised. The assumption that something esoteric or transcendental must be far off or complicated has been assumed by the ignorance of individuals. And that kind of individual is the least qualified to judge the matter. It is 'far off' only in a direction which he does not realise.'

CHAPTER ELEVEN

Gurdjieff, enemy of sleep

There can be no doubt that it was the work of George Ivanovitch Gurdjieff to make a very significant contribution to the esoteric education and development of Western man, or more accurately, a number of Western men and women, during the first half of the twentieth century. He died in 1949, having helped, by his great abilities and truly remarkable efforts, his students to shake off some of their sleep and to increase their consciousness.

Nevertheless, his disciples recognised by common assent that not one of them had reached that state of full awakening that they had sought, and which was the ultimate object of his teaching.

Thus no successor to Gurdjieff was, or indeed could be, appointed. Whether by intention or accident, the teaching was incomplete. Without the teacher nothing further could be done.

However, some of his students did not recognise that, despite Gurdjieff's clear warnings and indications on the subject, either appointing themselves or accepting others as 'teachers'. But the more discerning of them realised that their only hope of further progress lay in finding and contacting the Source which had educated and sent them Gurdjieff.

This they then attempted to do for the next ten years through individuals and search parties wandering vainly around the East with an increasing sense of desperation, meeting guru after guru, and many an apparent sage. But to no avail. None of these persons showed any indication of possessing or being connected with the teaching presented by Gurdjieff. They failed to find the Source. But then, in 1962, when they had almost given up the search, the Source found *them*.

To authenticate this statement, and for its own intrinsic interest, let us look at what can be ascertained of Gurdjieff's life before his arrival in Moscow in 1912, and the formation, two years later in 1914, of his first group of pupils in that city, when it was joined by P.D. Ouspensky, the writer and thinker who was to become his best-known pupil.

George Ivanovich Gurdjieff was born in 1872 in the little town of Alexandropol in Armenia. His father was Greek and his mother Armenian. He was soon to be joined by a brother and four sisters. Of this cultural environment Ernest Scott writes, 'The Caucasus region has been a mixing bowl of cultures for thousands of years. European, Slavonic, Turkish, Roman, Mongol, Persian and even more ancient cultures have flooded into this area, and then receded, each leaving some contribution. It was into this fusion of influences that Gurdjieff was born.'*

But it was his father, a living representative of this rich and ancient culture as an able bard and storyteller 'in his day very popular among the inhabitants of the Transcaucasia and Asia Minor', who knew and recited legends of remote antiquity, including some, like the story of Gilgamesh, from Sumerian and Babylonian times, who Gurdjieff recognised and respected as his most profound early influence. 'My personal relationship to him was not as towards a father, but as towards an elder brother; and he, by his constant conversation with me and his extraordinary stories, greatly assisted the arising in me of poetic images and high ideals.'—so he tells us in his autobiographical book, 'Meetings with Remarkable Men'. Having explained what he means by 'a remarkable man', Gurdjieff says:

> Since the first such man I knew—whose influence left its trace
> on the whole of my life—was my father, I shall begin with him.

---

*'The People of the Secret' Ernest Scott.

There stands out in my memory all the grandeur of my father's calm and the detachment of his inner state in all its external manifestations, throughout the misfortunes that befell him.' and despite these misfortunes, '… he continued then as before, in all the difficult circumstances of life, to retain the soul of a true poet … in spite of the fact that he often happened to find himself in the midst of events beyond the control of man and resulting in all sorts of human calamities, and despite almost always encountering baser manifestations from the people around him—he did not lose heart, never identified himself with anything, and remained inwardly free and always himself.

And finally Gurdjieff recalls, 'What most displeased him was to be disturbed in the evening when he would sit in the open looking at the stars.'

Gurdjieff was fortunate indeed to have had this remarkable man as his father. But perhaps such matters are not merely under fortune's way.

At any rate, whether by accident or design, but indubitably responding to a call from deep within his own individuality, on reaching youth 'Gurdjieff became obsessed with the idea that there was a purpose and aim behind human life and that was hardly ever glimpsed in the ceaseless generations of man.'—as Ernest Scott subtly expresses it. Somewhere on the planet was knowledge, hidden knowledge, the knowledge of man's place and possible place in the Universe, and seek it he must.

He met others consumed with the same desire as himself. Calling themselves 'The Seekers of Truth', they set out on an unremitting search for this esoteric knowledge, 'the real and universal knowledge' of human potentiality and purpose, in whose existence they firmly and deeply believed.

Sometimes singly, sometimes in groups they undertook expeditions over a wide area of the East and Middle East. Gurdjieff mentions journeys across the Amu Darya, originally the Oxus, to Bokhara, Samarkand and Tashkent, to India and Tibet. They experienced many vicissitudes, and endured all kinds of hardships. Some of his colleagues died, others disappeared.

But finally, at the end of years of searching, with the help of a dervish guide who escorted him on a journey in which he was blindfolded for twelve days, except to cross difficult and dangerous ravines, having also taken an oath not to try to discover where he was going, Gurdjieff at last found what he was looking for. This was a monastery inhabited by a special community of men and women, engaged in work of particular importance to both the planet and themselves.

Gurdjieff was admitted to this monastery as a pupil. To his joy, he met there one of 'The Seekers of Truth', a certain prince, his special friend, who had found his way there before him. They are both convinced that this is the place and these are the people they had for so long been searching for. However, beyond describing certain sacred dances of extraordinary sophistication and of very great antiquity performed by highly trained priestess-dancers, in which 'one could read one or another truth placed there thousands of years before', Gurdjieff tells us little else about the monastery or what he learned there—except, significantly as we shall see, that its leader was a 'sheik'.

There is now cumulative evidence to suggest that this was, in fact, a Sufi monastery, but of a very special Order, and not one necessarily known to the generality of orders who call themselves by the name 'Sufi'. It appears that Gurdjieff had contacted a body of people who one might rightly regard as the inner Sufis, and evidence indicates that this was one of their centres somewhere in the Hindu Kush.

In order to validate this statement we must first return to Gurdjieff's early days. In 'Meetings with Remarkable Men', Gurdjieff tells us that he had always been fascinated by the possibility that a certain ancient esoteric School called the 'Sarmoung Brotherhood' created in Babylonian times, might still exist. On one occasion, he and his friend and 'remarkable man', Pogossian, while digging in one of the underground passages below the ruins of the ancient capital of Armenia, Ani, about thirty miles from Alexandropol, discovered an old parchment document in what appeared to be the remains of a monastic cell. They struggled to translate what transpires to be a letter written in an earlier and unknown Armenian by a certain Father Arem to another monk, in which he mentions the continued existence, contemporary with the time of writing, of the Sarmoung Brotherhood. Gurdjieff describes the incident:

> What struck us most was the word Sarmoung, which we had come across several times in the book called 'Merkhavat'.

This word is the name of a famous esoteric school which, according to tradition, was founded in Babylon as far back as 2,500 BC, and which was known to have existed somewhere in Mesopotamia up to the sixth or seventh century AD; but about its further existence one could not obtain anywhere the least information.

This school was said to have possessed great knowledge, containing the key to many secret mysteries.

Many times had Pogossian and I talked of this school and dreamed of finding out something authentic about it, and now suddenly we found it mentioned in this parchment. We were greatly excited.

But apart from its name being mentioned, we discovered nothing else from this letter. We knew no more than before when and how this school arose, where it had existed or whether it might even still exist.

Now after many searching years, in this monastery at the end of a valley hidden among the mountains of the Hindu Kush, Gurdjieff's dream had come true. In 1965 the traveller Desmond Martin wrote an account in an English periodical of a visit he made to a certain monastery deep in the Hindu Kush, belonging to, he says, 'the Sarmoun Community'. This, he tells us, is a brotherhood and sisterhood '... established here in North Afghanistan for many centuries who appear to operate also in the world outside. The Sarmouni (the name means 'The Bees') have often been accused of being Christians in disguise, Moslem sectarians, or of harbouring even more ancient beliefs, derived, some say, from Babylonia. Others claim that their teaching has survived the Flood; but which flood I cannot say.'

The writer then goes on to describe '... an articulated tree, of gold and other metals, which seemed to me to be unbelievably beautiful and resembled a Babylonian work of art which I had seen in Baghdad Museum. It served to indicate postures assumed by dervishes in their Yoga-like exercises, which, performed to special music, they studied for self-development.'

Now Gurdjieff, in his account of the sacred dances, had described an object resembling a tree, which was used by the priestess dancers as a kind of template for their movements.

Then, most significantly for those at all familiar with Gurdjieff's teaching, the visitor records, 'On a wall faced with white marble, delineated in polished rubies, glowed the symbol of the community. This is the mystical 'No-Koonja', the ninefold Naqsch or 'Impress', an emblem I was later to see in various forms embroidered on clothes. This figure 'reaches for the innermost secrets of man,' I was informed.' It is known that Gurdjieff used in his work a special symbol, a circle divided in a particular way into nine parts, which he called 'the enneagram'.*

In March 1964, an article had appeared in 'The Times' in which a correspondent described a visit to an unusual monastery in the Hindu Kush. It was entitled *'Elusive Guardians of Ancient Secrets'*:

> There were about 200 permanent residents, occupied in crafts and certain pursuits not specified, the shaik explained. They did not regard themselves as primarily religious, but as the guardians and exponents of an ancient secret knowledge from which all human higher aspirations were ultimately derived in some unfamiliar way. They diffused this, it appeared, at intervals throughout the world, watched its progress and maintained their end of the activity, again not specified, as the impulse for which they were responsible worked its way through the generations.

The writer referred to this community as 'The People of the Inner Court', and said they had centres in Persia and Iraq, as well as in the Central Asian Highlands. He continued:

> They do no preaching, but circulate their message in a special way unfamiliar to this age, and again not specified. When pressed, the Mir admitted to their organising centres of study which often became usurped in course of time, becoming 'mere philosophical grinding mills.' Upon them, regrettably, but without doubt, there was a curse.

---

*Shah showed this to be the central symbol of a sequence of three. A context necessary for its full understanding. The enneagram is of course ignorantly abused by 'new age' cultists today.

The latter observation—that unless there is a real Teacher present the living stream of teaching ceases to flow—is constantly made by Sufis. For some reason, however, it is rarely registered. The explanation may lie in the widespread inability to recognise such a man or a woman. Nevertheless, even common sense—which has its use even to the seeker—is usually neglected in this process.

Finally O.M. Burke, in his very valuable and interesting book *'Among the Dervishes'* (published in 1973) in which he describes periods of living and studying among several ancient spiritual communities in the Near and Middle East, gives us further information. With reference to certain Sufis he has encountered in the Hindu Kush area of Afghanistan, he says, 'They are also known as the Sarmoon—a code-word for 'bee', a reference to one of their exercises.' He adds, 'There is the teaching that it is from here that the Sufi message must be diffused, and that it will have to be naturalised in each community.'

Apart from the intrinsic interest of the various material quoted, it enables us to ascertain that George Ivanovith Gurdjieff received his esoteric education from a teacher or teachers belonging to a body of people whom we can call the Sarmouni Sufis. Reliable information has also emerged in the course of the last thirty years that this community is identical with the tradition called the Khwajagan or Order of the Masters, and the inner Naqshbandi Order, also known as the Designers. The Sufi Directorate resides here. When O.M. Burke asks the Sufi authority Suleiman Bey about the origins of Sufism, he is told, 'The School called the Masters (al-Khwajagan) lies behind all Sufi manifestations. This gave rise in historical times to organisations which have been called Orders.'

It would seem, therefore, that Gurdjieff was an emissary of these People, with a particular role to perform. The question is—*what* was that role? Upon the answer to this question depends the way one should view the attempts to perpetuate his teaching since his death about fifty years ago by the many 'Gurdjieff' groups in different parts of the West today.

There can be no doubt that Gurdjieff was a genuine teacher sent out to perform a certain tasks by the Inner Circle of humanity of which he sometimes spoke, and whose agent he was, at least from 1914 when he formed his first group in Moscow to when he died in 1949 in Paris. He was greatly respected by the men and women of unusual intelligence and integrity who lived and worked with him, and having personally known three of his former pupils, I have no difficulty in accepting their view. They knew Gurdjieff as an able master and remarkable man, and were convinced that those who seriously strove to develop themselves under his guidance did in fact do so.

But they were also convinced that despite long and hard efforts, not one of his students had acquired that state of full consciousness which they sought as the object of the teaching, by the time of Gurdjieff's death—or, more accurately, departure from this particular plane of life.

Realising that there was no possibility of proceeding without a teacher, these and other people close to Gurdjieff devoted their efforts over the following ten-year period, 1951 to 1961, to finding the Source which had educated and sent Gurdjieff, and without whose direction no further progress could be achieved. But in the end, as has been said, it was the Source that was to find them, or rather those still capable of being 'found' and of recognising the different mode of teaching it now projected. The timing of the new phase was a matter for the Source—in accordance with the requirements of 'the time, the place, and the people.'

It then became clear to the more alert and discerning of the ex-students of Gurdjieff that his work and task was merely of a preparatory nature. Others, however, proved quite incapable of assimilating this fact, so identified had they become with the mode of teaching they were familiar with, and which they therefore wished to retain, come what may—even if that which was to come should be the liberating truth.

Yet as far back as 1916, in Moscow, Gurdjieff himself had sought to alert this pupils to certain peculiar characteristics of the teaching he represented, which he called 'The Fourth Way'. Speaking of 'ways' he said:

> Two or three thousand years ago there were other ways which no longer exist and the ways now in existence were not so divided, they stood much closer one another.
>
> The fourth way differs from the old and the new ways by the fact that is it never a permanent way. It has no definite forms and there are no institutions connected with it. It appears and disappears, governed by some peculiar law of its own.

> The fourth way is never without some *work* of a definite significance, is never without some *undertaking* around which and in connection with it can alone exist. When this work is finished, that is to say, when the aim set before it has been accomplished, the fourth way disappears, that is, it disappears from the given place, disappears in its given form, continuing perhaps in another place in another form. Schools of the fourth way exist for the needs of the work that is being carried out in connection with the proposed undertaking. They never exist by themselves as schools for the purpose of education and instruction.

The significance of that message from the master does not appear to have been grasped or even registered by the remnant and derelict so-called Gurdjieff groups that are still with us today, and doubtless will be with us tomorrow.

But now and again a discriminating voice is heard from someone who has become disconnected with the activities perpetuated in the name of Gurdjieff. One such is Robert de Ropp:

> No matter how powerful the teacher, his followers can always be trusted to bring his world to a halt. This they generally do by creating a cult of personality around the teacher himself, and fossilising everything in exactly the form it was given. Using this fossilised teaching, they engage in mechanical repetitions of certain patterns of behaviour, assuring themselves and each other that they will attain liberation and higher consciousness as long as they never, never make the slightest change in anything the master taught.

> But life is change, and what is appropriate for one period is not necessarily valid for another. So all this effort to hold on to certain forms only results in the arrest of development. So another teacher has to appear, smash the fossil and start all over again.

Another such voice is that of Kathleen Riordan Speeth, who asks:

> Is there a living tradition imbued with that ineffable ingredient that subtly blesses human transformation, or has the work become an empty husk, a testament to what was, and is no more?

It should be apparent by now that there *is* indeed a living Tradition, but one which is no longer connected with the 'Gurdjieff' work, which in certain important respects must undeniably be regarded as 'an empty husk'.

Authentic clarification of the situation had in fact been available since as early as 1966 when Rafael Lefort received the following information from Sheik Hassan Effendi in Jerusalem:

> Gurdjieff was to teach certain things for a certain circumstance. That his teaching was to be adulterated and carried out long after it effectiveness was gone, under circumstances which were in any case changed, was inevitable and predictable. His role was a preparative one.

Later in Istanbul, another authority, Pir Daud, advised:

> If you seek knowledge you must be in tune with the developmental work that takes into consideration the circumstances and needs of the time ... These may constantly change, and thus the director of the activity must be constantly in touch with the main plan of activity.

When these statements were first published in Lefort's 'The Teachers of Gurdjieff', some heeded, but others remained curiously immune to their intelligence.

In this perspective, let us now attempt to look at the teaching of Gurdjieff with the intention of identifying certain ideas and aspects of his work which appear to be of enduring value and significance.

All who knew anything of George Ivanovitch Gurdjieff would concur that this man was truly the arch-enemy of sleep. That is—the sleep we sleep without knowing, the trance we tread in unaware. His constant aim was to shake us from this sleep so that we could begin to awake. But first he had to teach people that they *were* asleep, to disturb them from the deadliest of all dreams—that they were awake. Otherwise, of course, nothing further could be done.

It was for this reason that Gurdjieff constantly called people's attention to the fact that they do not 'remember themselves', that they do not possess what they imagine they possess—that state of consciousness of self or self-consciousness. This can only be a contribution of singular significance to our knowledge of ourselves. And a further significance lies in the fact that access to high consciousness is through the acquisition of this state.

> Man's possibilities are very great. You cannot conceive even a shadow of what man is capable of attaining. But nothing can be obtained in sleep.

Gurdjieff made it clear that nothing could be attained without both expert help and hard work. For 'the way of the development of hidden possibilities is a way *against nature*.' Nature includes human nature as it ordinarily is, in its unrefined state, with its freight of mostly unrecognised sleep-compelling habits. These habits had to be recognised and removed. Upon this depended the liberation and growth of the inner self, which Gurdjieff, like the Sufis, called 'the essence', which had to emerge and gradually permeate the whole being, dominating and controlling what he called 'the personality'. Though this is not necessarily personality as usually understood.

A 'way' was essential. 'The ways are narrow and straight. But at the same time only by them can anything be attained. The ways are opposed to everyday life ... The idea of the ways cannot be understood if one believes in the possibility of man's evolution without their help.'

Such evolution, Gudjieff emphasised, entails a parallel and integrated development of knowledge and being. 'The level of a man's knowledge depends on the level of his being,' he said. In other words, he cannot *know* more than he *is*. Knowledge and being are organically fused. They correspond, and ascend together. There is thus a hierarchy of being-knowledge. 'Within the limits of a given level of being the quality of knowledge cannot be changed.' Therefore, 'A change in the nature of knowledge is only possible with a change in nature of being.' So higher knowledge requires, can only be received by, can only be 'inherited' by, a transformation of very being.

And, asks Gurdjieff, 'What knowledge can a sleeping man have? His being prevents it. His being asleep prevents it.'

Both a cause and an aspect of man's sleep, according to Gurdieff, was his lack of presence, his lack of presence *in* himself, his lack of presence *unto* himself. 'Life is real only then when I am,' he said, which could also be put, 'Only when I am is life real.' To *be*, to fully *be*, to really *be*, is a great achievement, connected clearly with the state of self-remembering or self-consciousness. Caught up 'in the rushing stream of things' as the philosopher Porphyry described it, we mostly drift through life, unpresent, unconscious of, and absent from ourselves. Engulfed in events or immersed in our daydreams, we are oblivious of the fact that we are not really *here* most of time, not really 'at home' for longer periods than we imagine—so unconscious of our very unconsciousness are we!

In this regard Gurdjieff called attention to a characteristic tendency we all have, but are unaware of, which he termed 'identification'. This is the constant and for the most part unconscious proclivity to be caught up in, attached to, taken over by, events, circumstances, states of mind, all kinds of involvements inner and outer, with which we 'identify', losing one's self in the particular situation or state. We then become the victim of the event, whatever it is. Of ourselves little, if anything, remains. Once one becomes aware of the pervasive and pernicious nature of identification, one can understand why Gurdjieff said, 'Identifying is the chief obstacle to self-remembering. A man who identifies with anything is unable to remember himself.'

And so the practice of 'non-identifying', of retaining one's sense of self, of maintaining one's presence in the centre of centrifugal things, was a necessary complement to the practice of self-remembering.

Gurdjieff further warned that one had to be particularly careful not to identify with 'oneself'—that is all that is not one's real self, but which postures, often very convincingly, as such. One has to be discriminatingly alert to recognise and outwit this false self. In Gurdjieff's words:

> In order to remember oneself it is necessary first of all not to identify. But in order to learn not to identify a man must first of all not be identified with himself, must not call himself 'I' always and on all occasions. He must remember that there are two in him, that there is himself, that is 'I' in him, and there is *another* with whom he must struggle and whom he must conquer if he wishes at any time to attain anything. So long as a man identifies or can be identified, he is the slave of everything that can happen to him. Freedom is first of all freedom from identification.

This, like so much of what Gurdjieff taught, is surely a contribution of very great value to our knowledge of the human condition. Only those content to remain asleep and who fear (rightly!) a threat to their slumber will fail to see it. Willing victims of the Hypnotist, addicts of amnesia, nothing can disturb their dreamless sleep!

Nevertheless, something which has not been sufficiently grasped by those not impervious to his words is that not everything Gurdjieff said was meant to be taken as literally true. A number of his statements were deliberately provocative remarks issued to his students for teaching purposes, rather than the truths of a teaching. In other words, they were 'technical' rather than factual. Unfortunately, what were in reality delivered as shocks to stir a sleeper or sleepers on a certain occasion, have all too often become enshrined as absolute truths. Gurdjieff here showed the influence of the Sufi masters he had met, who however employ techniques of provocation in a more sophisticated way.

We must take our hats off to the great Mr. G., whose whole life was an extraordinary and extended effort of inner service to mankind. But we must also remember that he said, 'I am small compared to those that sent me.'*

---

*Recorded in 1946 by his pupil Charles Nott in 'Diary of a Pupil'.

CHAPTER TWELVE

The way of the sufi

Sufism is an ancient yet timeless Teaching, which, according to its custodians, has always been with us in one form or another. Its origin can either be regarded as lost in the mists of antiquity, operating in forgotten cultures we know not of, or, more truly, always above and always within, emerging from eternity, from the timeless, from time to time, into time. 'Our wine existed before the grape and the vine' claims the Sufi poet Ibn el-Farid; while the master Hujwiri in his classic eleventh century text, 'Revelation of the Veiled' maintains: 'Sufism has no history as other things have a history. It can be said to have existed always.'

Sufism, therefore, is not 'Islamic mysticism'. It existed before the coming and outside the confines of Islam. It would be more correct to say that Islamic mysticism is simply a particular, culturally-oriented, projection of Sufism. 'Sufism has been known under many names, to all peoples from the beginning of human times.' states the contemporary Sufi master and historian, Idries Shah. 'The Sufi entity is a community and an organism ... Its function as a school and a leaven in societies has enabled it to develop and flourish again and again in the most diverse cultures.' Shah here calls attention to an important and subtle concept. The Sufi school is an *organism*, not an

79

organisation. It works as a living leaven hidden and growing in the very heart of a culture, infusing and influencing it from within. We recall that Jesus uses the same metaphor: 'The kingdom of heaven is like leaven ...' (Matthew 13:33).

On the perennity and variety of the teaching's manifestations Sufis concur. The authority Suhrawardi of the twelfth century, in his colossal *'Wisdom of Illumination'*, specifically states: 'the Sufi philosophy is identical with the inner teaching of all the ancients—the Egyptians, the Persians, the Greeks—and is the Knowledge of Light and the deepest truth, through which man can attain to a status about which he can normally not even dream.'

In the following century, the English Sufi Roger Bacon endorses this in his 'Philosophia Occulta'. This knowledge, he says, 'was known to Noah and Abraham, to the Chaldean and Egyptian masters, to Zoroaster and Hermes, to certain Greeks including Pythagoras, Anaxagoras and Socrates, and to the Sufis.' In this sense, he avers, they are all Sufis.

It is therefore true to say that Sufism is the 'the Teaching behind all teachings'. It is a tradition, but one which is constantly maintained from and sustained by an extra-dimensional source. Its planetary centre is thus ultimately connected with a cosmic and divine impulse, which it receives and serves. Its members are 'The Permanent Staff on Earth' of a Cosmic Community. At the same time, they are members of the planetary human community, with which they have indissoluble bonds, and which they have served and guided since the beginning of its existence on earth. It is for such reasons that it is rightly said, 'The Sufi is the Friend of Man'; and why Sufis themselves insist, 'The Way is none other than in the service of the people.'

In fact the Sufi needs society as much as society needs the Sufi. For it is through his involvement with society, with his fellow human beings, that the Sufi grows, and achieves the development he seeks. He must 'be *in* the world but not *of* the world.'—a traditional requisite of this path. In the words of Akbar Khan in his 'Tasawuf-i-Azim':

> Man is destined to live a social life. His part is to be with other human beings. In serving Sufism he is serving the Infinite, serving himself, and serving society. He cannot cut himself from any

one of these obligations and become or remain a Sufi. The only discipline worthwhile is that which is achieved in the midst of temptation. A man who, like the anchorite, abandons the world and cuts himself off from temptations and distractions cannot achieve power. For power is that which is won through being wrested from the midst of weakness and uncertainty. The ascetic living wholly a monastic life is deluding himself.

There we have it. A most significant statement by the seventeenth century master. But there is more to it than that. For the role of 'the world', the complex environment through which one moves, to which one relates, and in which, to a certain extent at any rate, one has one's being, in fact contains developmental possibilities for the follower of this Way very much more various and subtle than this authority has here chosen to communicate. Another master has said, 'For the Sufi the world is a fashioning instrument.' By which he means that it is, in every sense, a 'growing medium'.

But because of the presence of the Sufi in its midst, the leaven hidden within it, the whole community benefits. His influence in fact goes further. Shah explains:

> To the Sufi, the evolution of the Sufi is within himself and also in relationship with society. The development of the community, and the destiny of all creation—even nominally inanimate creation—is interwoven with the destiny of the Sufi. He may have to detach himself for a period from society—a moment, a month, even more—but ultimately he is interlinked with the eternal whole. The Sufi's importance, therefore, is immense, and his actions and appearance to others will seem to vary with human and extrahuman needs.

Man, say the Sufis, is part of the Eternal Whole, from which everything is derived, and to which all must return. This requires a certain kind of purification and process of perfection leading ultimately to the Complete Man. It requires the cultivation of, as dervishes of the Bektashi Order call it, 'The Intelligence of Return'.

But where does the Return Journey begin? It begins, it *must* begin, exactly *here*, where one is, in the culture in which one lives, and by which one has been formed, shaped and influenced. And within that culture in the very situation one is actually in. It starts where you are—*now*.

Clearly the journey can only be effected with the help of a school specially designed for such a purpose by experts who thoroughly understand the culture—its vices, virtues and capacities, and also those of the individual prospective traveller.

An authentic school must organically connect with the culture concerned and with the higher level of being beyond. This indeed has always been a distinguishing feature of the genuine Sufi entity, which is never created without sensitive observance of 'the time, the place, and the people'. The school founded here in the West by Idries Shah in 1963 patently manifests this quality, while at the same time clearly indicating a living connection to the whole Sufic tradition. We must therefore give it our attention.

Shah himself belongs to a most ancient and distinguished family known and respected throughout the Middle East as 'the People of the House'. From time to time, often at important historical moments, this Family, who appear to be custodians of a secret inner tradition, produce members with a special mission to perform. Thus Jalaluddin Rumi, Bahaudin Naqshband, Sheikh Shattar, and other great mystical masters, were of this line.

For some time, apparently over several generations, this Family has been focusing its attention on the West, with a view to Sufic educational intervention. Shah's father, the Sirdar Ikbal Ali Shah, a remarkable man, highly regarded wherever he went—writer, scholar, traveller and diplomat—devoted his life to developing a line of spiritual communication between the East and the West, and was undoubtedly a great influence and inspiration in preparing his son, Idries, for his work.

Shah indeed eminently evinces that understanding of the culture in all its idiosyncrasies, which Sufis deem so necessary for their undertakings. Though truly Afghan by origin, he is at the same time more English than the English, with a virtuoso command of the language, ranging consummately across a wide and deep diapason of expression. Though always his inimitable self, it is to the great Tradition he represents that he constantly draws our attention, introducing us to the colossal Sufi heritage of stories, poems, statements, and sayings. Through him the past masters become present. But it is upon the teaching rather than the teacher that we must concentrate. 'Look not at my face, but take what is in my hand,' says Rumi. Through the rich and resonant literature Idries Shah has collected and contributed to, one senses a tree of living Wisdom, with roots in the most remote past yet ever pressing its leaves into the present.

In particular, he has presented to us a large number of those special and subtle entities traditionally studied by inner schools of Sufis, which they call 'teaching stories'. These are indeed jewels from the Sufi Treasury, to which Shah has apparently unlimited access, and are a distinctive feature of the teaching mode of his school. However, it must be clearly understood that the tales are only a part of a larger teaching operation, a whole to which they are organically related. Though the reader can enjoy and benefit from them as 'literature', they are certainly not literature as normally understood. They are in fact 'work material' with internal dimensions that can only be unlocked and revealed in the course of this work. They are 'operational' texts that can only be fruitfully studied within a whole and authentic teaching context, by a serious student, under genuine guidance. It is very likely that the parables of Jesus are of this nature. Moreover, it is significant to observe that a number of these are in current use by present masters of the Sufi Way.

How then should the Sufi stories be approached by those seriously interested in what they can yield?

Firstly with humility—which means a state of open-ness, of accessibility, of calm yet alert receptivity to whatever there *is* to be received. Seek not to impose upon, or wrest interpretations, from the story. Be *available* to it—fully and wholly available. 'Let the tale tell *you* what *it* means'* the poet Pamela Travers wisely advises. The tales may not so much mean something for you as *do* something *to* you. So *let* them act. Simply absorb them. 'Let them seep into your mind,' says Shah. Deep within you they will have their effect slowly and surely, 'as a seed growing secretly' as Jesus described this process, gradually awakening your inner consciousness.

For the tales contain deep dimensions that can only be contacted and entered deeply—which means openly and sensitively, allowing

---

* The Sufi, Hafiz Amir, tells us: 'It yields successive meanings from time to time in accordance with the level of insight it itself has helped to develop.'

them to reach and exert their impact upon, that deeper part of ourselves with which they communicate. With regard to the teaching story, Shah says, 'Its action is upon the innermost part of the human being … It establishes in him or her a means of communication with a truth beyond the customary limitations of our familiar dimensions.'

Sidney Spencer, author of the classic work, 'Mysticism in World Religion', offers, in an article on the work of Idries Shah, his own valuable observation:

> The teaching story springs from, and makes its appeal to, the inner and greater self that lies, as the Sufis (like all mystics) maintain, beyond the normal and superficial self, which is blind to its own deeper being. The stories are calculated to bring into play, perhaps by their very strangeness and unexpectedness, the forces of the hidden life.

Spencer expresses considerable insight into the nature and effect of the Dervish story. They are indeed highly sophisticated and conscious works of art, created by people who knew exactly what they were doing, for the help of others willing to align themselves with their influence. The purpose, according to Shah, of these 'tales formed according to a Design' is to provide 'a framework for the reception of the illumination'. They are subtly complex creations capable of acting simultaneously in many ways and on many levels. They have various roles. Some show us the nature and inadequacies of certain usual patterns of thought which we have without being aware of them, while at the same time revealing other possibilities. Others move us along unfamiliar pathways of the mind in order to open them up. As a body, and rightly used, they offer 'a way into another form of being.'

Here then is such a teaching story, from Idries Shah's 'Tales of the Dervishes', followed by the note which he provides:

The idiot, the wise man, and the jug

An idiot may be the name given to the ordinary man, who consistently misinterprets what happens to him, what he does, or what is brought about by others. He does this so completely plausibly that—for himself and his peers—large areas of his life and thought seem logical and true.

An idiot of this kind was sent one day with a pitcher to a wise man, to collect some wine.

On the way the idiot, through his own heedlessness, smashed the jar against a rock.

When he arrived at the house of the wise man, he presented him with the handle of the pitcher and said, 'So-and-so sent you this pitcher, but a horrid stone stole it from me.'

Amused and wishing to test his coherence, the wise man asked, 'Since the pitcher is stolen, why do you offer me the handle?'

'I am not such a fool as people say,' the idiot told him, 'and therefore I have brought the handle to prove my story.'

NOTE: A recurrent theme among the dervish teachers is that humanity generally cannot distinguish a hidden trend in events which alone would enable it to make full use of life. Those who can see this thread are termed the Wise; while the ordinary man is said to be 'asleep', or called the Idiot.

This story, quoted in English by Colonel Wilberforce Clarke (Diwan-i-Hafiz) is a typical one. The contention is constructive: that by absorbing this doctrine through such caricatures, certain human beings can actually 'sensitise' themselves for the perception of the hidden trend.

The present extract is from a dervish collection attributed to Pir-i-do-Sara, 'The Wearer of the Patchwork Robe', who died in 1790 and is buried at Mazar-i-Sharif in Turkistan.

These stories resonate with harmonic inner tones. Read and re-read them in patience. For from patience comes perception. The perception to perceive the very Thread of Ariadne.

The teaching stories are very important. Nevertheless, as has been said, they constitute only one aspect of the whole, which is the study of Sufism. As elements in a total organic teaching situation, they can only be fully activated *within* this situation, and according to the corresponding degree of preparation and development of the student.

For the Way of the Sufi is infinitely individual. We are all wonderfully different, so we must all tread our own particular and personal path—which is nevertheless somehow subsumed within the wider Path. As the Sufis say, 'There are as many ways to Truth as there are human souls.' And how else *could* it be?

The Sufi way passes *through* the world. It is intricately intermeshed with the very texture of our terrestrial existence. As each of us and our lives is unique, so is our unfolding. We learn in our *own* way *in* the Way. The Teaching both exposes our concealed faults and discloses our hidden talents. Sometimes gently, sometimes roughly, we are revealed to ourselves and enabled to grow. Gradually we begin to see our Life manifesting through life. The world becomes more and more transparent to Reality.

And who knows, but on some ordinary day, when you least expect it, you will glimpse Khidr, the mysterious Guide of the Sufis. He might brush past you in the rush hour; or greet you in a garden. As well could he whisper at your ear in the bus queue, as beckon from the setting sun.

He has something to say to you—and to you alone. For the purpose of Sufism is to make you really *you*. No one *else* can possibly do!

For why did God create us? He desired good company—interesting, creative company—a little like Himself. So *make* yourselves interesting, Ladies and Gentlemen. Whatever you do, don't *bore* the Lord! Or, for that matter, *yourselves*!

He began us, but He didn't complete us. That He has left for us to do—should we so desire. We now have the opportunity to *participate* in our own further creation. Without this, without *us*, it cannot be done.

As the Sufi Saadi of Shiraz says:

> Deep in the sea are riches beyond compare.
>
> But if you seek safety, it is on the shore.

Or, as Sean O'Casey puts it: 'Life is an *invitation* to living.'

ESOTERICISM

Thank God for esotericism and the secret things
Hid in the common light we think is day:
The ordinary gate that should you know it swings
Open to Eden from the builder's yard;
The abandoned ladder that's the stairway to the stars.
Thank God for those who even yet can tell
Where below brambles lies the long lost well.
For us who live in this world pale and pall –
Thank God there is a Secret after all!

FURTHER READING

Burke, O.M., *Among the Dervishes*. London, Octagon Press. The record of a remarkable journey to the East and Middle East in which the traveller visits ancient spiritual communities where he learns about matters of importance to mankind. Of particular interest is his encounter with a school of esoteric Christians claiming a direct link with Jesus, and a different understanding of his teachings.

Daumal, René, *Mount Analogue*. France, Gallimard. London, Vincent-Stuart. Daumal's masterwork extraordinaire. The 'authentic narrative' of an expedition to climb a mountain compared to which Everest is a mere foothill—Mount Analogue. 'A way that unites Heaven and Earth, which must exist, otherwise our situation would be without hope.' Not for the plains-dweller.

Gorman, Max, Jesus the Sufi. Crucible Publishers. Identifies Jesus as a teacher in the Sufi tradition, with a wealth of parables and sayings, known and unknown. (For more information see www.maxgorman.net)

Lefort, Rafael, *The Teachers of Gurdjieff*. London, Gollancz. An exciting quest for the source of Gurdjieff's teaching, a travel story dramatically unfolding—but whose real value lies in the wisdom that is encountered en route. Both the author, and the reader who accompanies him, are enriched on this unusual journey.

Quispel, G. (Translator), *The Gospel According to Thomas*. London, Collins. Discovered in the sands of Egypt near Nag Hammadi, this invaluable 2nd Century document consists of a large number of parables and sayings of Jesus, known and unknown. It brings into view an essentially mystical Christianity, and Jesus as an exponent of an ancient wisdom tradition.

Scott, Ernest, *The People of the Secret*. London, Octagon Press. A unique study of the possible influence upon human affairs of a 'Hidden Directorate', whose purpose is to guide the evolution of man, in harmony with a Cosmic Plan. The Author traces the pattern of such intervention over a wide range of human history with verve and virtuosity.

Shah, Idries, *The Way of the Sufi*. London, Octagon Press. A rich and varied anthology of Sufi philosophy, poetry, stories and sayings, from masters of the Path, offering an introduction to the current phase of the teaching.

Shah, Idries, *Tales of the Dervishes*. London, Octagon Press. Teaching-stories from the Sufi Treasury, resonating with harmonics of the highest level—they teach, transmit and transform.

Wilson, Colin, *The War Against Sleep*. England, Aquarian Press. A spirited study of Gurdjieff, benefiting from the lively and individual observations of the Author, who has clearly been much influenced himself by the master.